Heinemann Explore Science

Teacher's Book

New International Edition

Grade 6

Tara Lievesley, Deborah Herridge
Series editor: John Stringer

ALWAYS LEARNING

PEARSON

Pearson Education Limited is a company incorporated in England and Wales having its registered office at Edinburgh Gate, Harlow, Essex, CM20 2JE.

Registered company number: 872828

Text © Pearson Education Limited 2012
First published 2003. This edition published 2012.

www.pearsonglobalschools.com

16 15 14 13 12
IMP 10 9 8 7 6 5 4 3 2 1

British Library Cataloguing in Publication Data
A catalogue record for this book is available from the British Library

ISBN 978 0 43513 368 9

Edited by Glenys Davis
Designed by Techset Ltd, Gateshead
Original illustrations © Pearson Education Limited, 2003, 2009, 2012
Illustrated by TechSet Ltd, Gateshead
Cover photo/illustration © Alamy Images
Printed in China (SWTC/01)

Acknowledgements
Every effort has been made to contact copyright holders of material reproduced in this book. Any omissions will be rectified in subsequent printings if notice is given to the publishers.

Contents

Introduction

Heinemann Explore Science New International Edition provides a comprehensive, easy-to-use resource written especially for the international primary classroom.

The teaching framework follows the Cambridge International Examinations Primary Science Curriculum Framwork (2011), enabling you to minimize planning. The simple structure of *Heinemann Explore Science* gives you flexibility to teach the Units within a Grade in the order that suits your situation.

There is one Unit for each half of a term, with multiple lessons in that Unit. However, Grade 6 includes three shorter Units to the same general format. The first lesson in each Unit is an introduction and the last one is a plenary. The other lessons either focus on knowledge and understanding or on manageable, tried and tested investigation activities. The greater the opportunity for investigation, the more practical lessons there are.

Each Grade of *Heinemann Explore Science* contains in the *Teacher's Book* detailed teacher's notes, which provide all the resources you need for planning and delivering successful science lessons. It also includes an accompanying *Student Book* to bring the science topics to life for the children; a *Workbook* with activities to do at school or at home, and six *Readers* to develop students' English language skills through science. Alongside these components, digital resources available via online subscription provide an e-book version of the printed books, opportunities for independent research into the Biology, Chemistry and Physics covered in the scheme and further activities and simulations. For more information on digital resources for this course, visit www.pearsonglobalschools.com/explorescience.

This unique combination of science and ICT stimulates students and enables you to deliver enriching science lessons using today's technology.

Heinemann Explore Science and English language development

Science and language development have much in common. In both, students are frequently highly motivated. Science is a popular subject area in primary schools with students (and with teachers!), and produces interesting and engaging results. Language and science are both social activities. Students' language will not develop without co-operation and collaboration, and science is also a collaborative subject. Finally, science experiences can lead, as few other subjects do, to a desire to communicate discoveries.

When developing spoken English, remember:

- Discussion can be stimulated by working in threes. Two friends doing science may have a common and familiar way of communicating. Three extends the discussion.

- Snowball or jigsaw activities, in which groups share and exchange information, are engaging.

- Discussion before and after an investigation can clarify thoughts. Having to explain what students discovered in their investigation helps clarify thinking and improve language skills.

- Presenting results to others imposes a discipline as well as giving purpose to recording and to clear presentation.

- Reading can be developed through following instructions – including safety instructions – and using the *Student Book* and targeted *Readers*.

Students may be understandably reluctant to record their discoveries. When encouraging written recording, use a variety of recording methods.

- Writing to a structure helps to order students' thoughts.

- Annotated diagrams are an effective way of recording practical science – used by adult scientists as well as students.

- A recorded observation alone may lead to a conclusion.

- Ordering and recording whole investigations is difficult, and can often be better done to a writing framework.

Heinemann Explore Science offers and defines new vocabulary. If the words are new to you, or you have any doubts yourself about their definition, use the definitions in the Glossary in the *Student Book*.

- Draw the students' attention to the new words.

- Depending on the students' age, set them to illustrate or define the words themselves. Introduce word games – matching the word to the definition.

- Make a 'Words of Science' poster or a class dictionary.

- Ask the students to use the words in context; to act them out; to guess which word you are thinking of, either by 20 questions or by giving clues.

- Use cloze procedure to place new words.

Components of the scheme

The **Heinemann Explore Science** *Teacher's Book* provides detailed guidance on teaching with the corresponding sections of the *Student Book* pages. Used alongside the electronic components, where you will find a variety of resources for planning and teaching, the *Teacher's Book* is the main starting point for any lesson. Each Unit provides approximately a half-term's worth of work – an introduction, and almost always four lesson plans (each of which may be taught in a single session or across science sessions during the week), and a final review.

Each Unit introduction provides:

1 Clear background science information to support the non-specialist teacher.

2 Simple definitions of necessary scientific vocabulary.

3 A complete list of resources needed in the Unit.

4 Helpful hints on prior preparation or useful additional resources.

5 Indications of what students should already know and be able to do before starting the Unit.

6 Cross-curricular references to other subject areas.

7 A discussion question to set the scene and introduce a context for the Unit.

There are two types of lesson in **Heinemann Explore Science**. The first type focuses on knowledge and understanding objectives. These lessons contain:

1 Starter activities to initiate whole-class discussion. Questioning will enable you to establish what the students already know.

2 References to the corresponding *Student Book* pages and further information to expand on the paragraphs in the *Student Book*.

3 Safety tips to advise of specific hazards where appropriate.

4 Additional information necessary for the activities in the 'Things to do' section of the *Student Book*, plus suggestions of how to differentiate and record. Any worksheets required are cross-referenced.

5 Integrated ICT research activities using the website.

6 Further details or extra 'fun facts' to support those listed in the *Student Book*.

7 The answer to the 'I wonder...' question, with additional background explanation if necessary.

8 More activities that can be used instead of, or as well as, those in the 'Things to do' section.

9 Ideas for how students could present their work or tips for classroom displays are provided on the website to help students.

10 Suggestions for homework activities.

11 An activity or series of questions to reinforce the main objectives in the plenary session, drawing the lesson to a close.

The second type of lesson offers a challenge to encourage students to use scientific enquiry skills to investigate a problem in context. These contain:

1 Starter activities to initiate whole-class discussion.

2 A challenge introduced in context, explaining what students will be investigating.

3 Safety tips advising of unique hazards where appropriate; an individual risk assessment is always recommended.

4 Further details of how to carry out the investigation, supporting the instructions in the *Student Book*.

5 Lists of materials students will need, including any to be prepared in advance.

6 Explanations of what students should be looking for, or how to keep the test fair. How best to support and extend students.

7 How to organize, record, analyze and present data collected in the investigation. Suitable tables for data recording are provided as worksheets in the *Workbook*.

8 Students are encouraged to review how well they carried out their investigation and how good their results were. Using the report provided for each investigation helps students build evaluation skills by criticizing methods and conclusions.

9 A different scenario is offered to enable students to apply what they have learned.

10 Additional activities can be used instead of, or as well as, the investigative challenge.

11 Suggestions for homework activities.

12 An activity or series of questions to reinforce the main objectives in the plenary session draw the lesson to a close.

At the end of each Unit, material is provided for an assessment and review lesson:

1 A clear summary of the knowledge and skills students have gained through the Unit divided into three levels of attainment.

2 Explanation and expected responses to the 'Check-up' in the *Student Book*.

3 Answers to the assessment worksheets in the *Workbook*.

4 The answer to the original question posed at the beginning of the Unit.

5 A final activity completes the Unit and reminds students of everything they have learned.

In addition, there are six readers for each Grade of the Cirriculum Framework. These are written to match the appropriate science for the Grade, but with close attention to language levels. Students can learn English language through science, and science through practising their English.

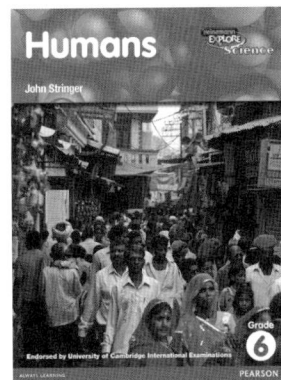

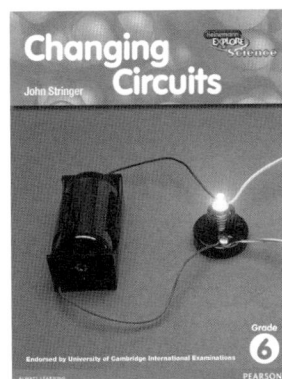

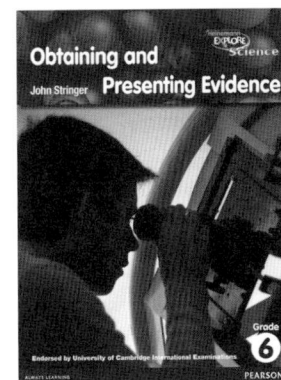

Quick guide to the *Teacher's Book*

The ***Heinemann Explore Science*** *Grade 6 Teacher's Book* provides detailed guidance on teaching with the corresponding *Student Book* pages. Used alongside the e-book, the *Teacher's Book* is the main starting point for any lesson. Each Unit provides approximately one half-term's worth of work and comprises an introduction and generally six or seven lessons (each of which may be taught all at once, or across a number of science sessions during the week), plus a review.

Each Unit introduction provides:

2 A complete list of resources needed throughout the unit.

3 Helpful hints on prior preparation or useful resources.

1 Clear background science information to support the non-specialist teacher.

4 Indicators of what students should know and be able to do before starting this Unit.

5 Specific references to other subject areas.

7 Useful definitions of scientific vocabulary commonly misunderstood by students.

6 An initial discussion question to set the scene and introduce a context for the Unit.

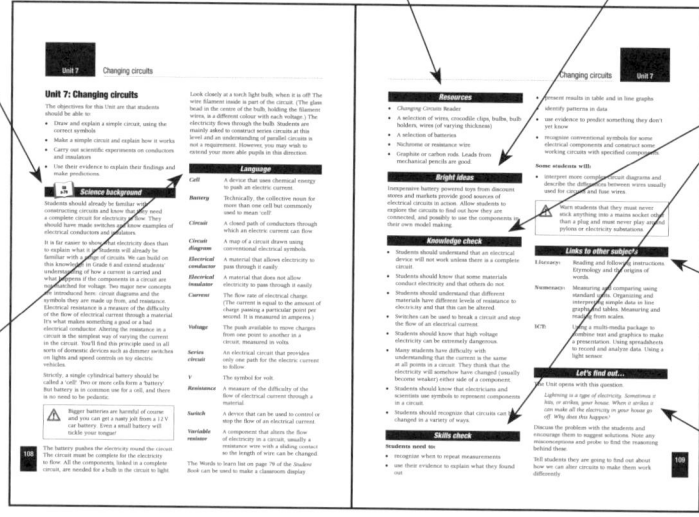

There are two types of lesson in *Heinemann Explore Science*. The first type focuses on knowledge and understanding objectives.

1 Starter activities initiate whole-class discussion. Questioning will enable you to find out what the students already know.

2 Safety tips warn of possible hazards where appropriate.

3 The answer to the 'I wonder...' question, with additional background explanation if necessary.

10 References to the corresponding *Student Book* pages and further information to expand on the paragraphs in the *Student Book*.

4 Ideas for how students could present their work or tips for classroom displays.

9 Any additional information necessary for the activities in the 'Things to do' section of the *Student Book*, plus suggestions of how to differentiate and record.

5 Suggestions for homework activities.

8 Further details or extra 'fun facts' to support those listed in the *Student Book*.

7 More activities that can be used instead of or as well as those in the 'Things to do' section.

6 An activity or series of questions to help reinforce the main objectives in the Plenary session to draw the lesson to a close.

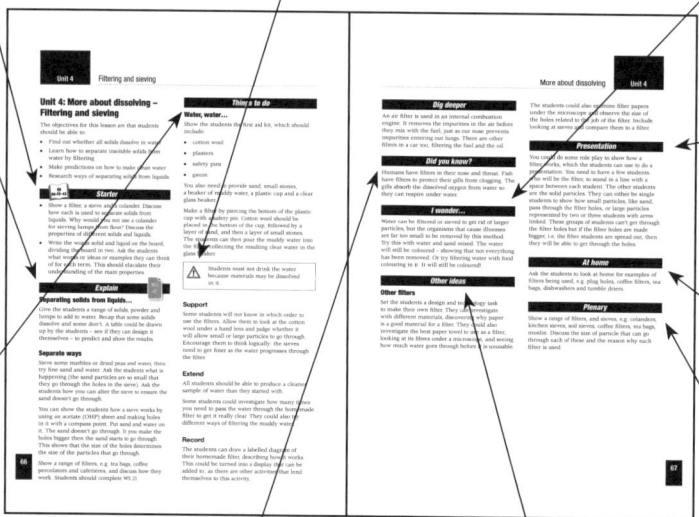

The second type of lesson offers a challenge to encourage students to use their scientific enquiry skills to investigate a problem in context.

1 Starter activities initiate whole-class discussion.

2 Safety tips warn of possible hazards where appropriate.

3 Information on how to organize, record, analyze and present data collected in the investigation. Spreadsheet tables for recording results and exemplar data to convert into charts or graphs can be found in the *Student Book* or *Workbook*.

12 The challenge introduces the context and explains what students will be investigating.

4 More activities that can be used instead of or as well as the investigative challenge.

11 Further details of how to carry out the investigation to support the instructions to the students in the *Student Book*.

5 Suggestions for homework activities.

10 List of materials that students will need, including any that need to be prepared in advance.

6 An activity or series of questions to help reinforce the main objectives in the Plenary session to draw the lesson to a close.

9 Explanations of what students should be looking for and noticing, or how they should keep the test fair. Ideas on how to support and extend students are also included.

8 Students are encouraged to review how well they carried out their investigation and how good their results were. Use the report provided for each investigation to help students build evaluation skills by criticizing methods and conclusions.

7 Present students with a different scenario to enable them to apply what they have learned.

At the end of each Unit, material is provided for an assessment and review lesson.

2 Assessment sheets can be found in the *Workbook*.

1 A clear summary of the knowledge and skills students have gained throughout the Unit.

3 A final activity completes the unit to remind students of everything they have learned.

5 Explanation and expected responses to the Check-up in the *Student Book*.

4 The answer to the original question posed at the beginning of the Unit. Discuss what the students think now in light of what they have learned.

How to use
Heinemann Explore Science

For ease of use, **Heinemann Explore Science** follows the structure of the Cambridge Primary Science Curriculum Framework, 2011. **Heinemann Explore Science** has been written so that you can be flexible about what you teach and when.

Heinemann Explore Science is more manageable than many primary science schemes. It has a simple structure, but it also offers wide investigative and research opportunities. A range of engaging tasks is offered for each topic, including practical and research-based activities. Its clear progression and layout offers more support to less confident teachers. Integrated assessment gives indications of how to interpret levels of attainment. There is support for differentiation with suggestions for extra challenges for bright students and support for students struggling with science concepts. There is both experimental and investigative science through reliable practical investigations.

Heinemann Explore Science emphasizes: investigations; the clear use of strong vocabulary lists; building on students' ideas and addressing common misconceptions through questioning and discussion; clearly identified support and extend activities; class demonstration as a basis for some practical activities; and appropriate activities as part of students' homework. It offers flexibility of use; although Units are ordered to match the Cambridge Curriculum Framework, they can be taught in any order to suit a school's own scheme of work. This helps in mixed-age classes.

Differentiation

Within any class there will be a wide range of experience and ability. In a mixed-age class that range is further extended. This is a challenge to any teacher, and many address it through careful differentiation. Commonly, work is planned for a number of different groups (often three: high achievers, a middle range group, and students needing additional support). Teachers then allocate their resources – human and practical – to these groups to ensure the best possible outcome for everybody. This 'planning for differentiation' is demanding, and may leave feelings of dissatisfaction – 'I didn't spend long enough with the high-fliers/slower group today', 'I hope I'm not neglecting the majority of the class'. Some teachers have similar difficulties with 'differentiation by outcome'. Less able students may be unchallenged by the assumption that they will always produce a few lines of text when others routinely write a page.

Heinemann Explore Science expects that you will need to differentiate your work, and so a range of resources is offered, any of which may stimulate particular groups. You may choose to: present an activity on an investigation table, possibly supported by an informed adult; to set out resources that students can use for creative play; or to use the *Student Book* or *Workbook* for stimulus, for direction or for recording.

The 'starting off' activities in **Heinemann Explore Science** invite a third form of differentiation: differentiation by presentation. This is so familiar to teachers that few recognize how effectively they use it. The way in which a topic is presented engages students, but it also enables you to assess their prior knowledge. Because of its practical nature, students who may not shine in other subjects will often contribute more in science. Students who are able in every respect may still surprise you with their knowledge, but this 'knowledge' needs to be probed carefully – a superficial knowledge may lack the depth of understanding on which new science learning can be built.

That's why **Heinemann Explore Science** includes a number of exemplar questions to elicit current understanding – whether it is insecure, or even whether students have misconceptions that need gently challenging. It is when you group the students and set the tasks that you 'differentiate by presentation' – an unconscious and instinctive skill that results in different groups busily engaged with differing levels of support and monitoring.

Level statements to help you identify at which level students are working are provided in this *Teacher's Book*, for each Unit. These are also provided at the back of the *Student Book* for discussion and as checklists to enable self-assessment by students.

Heinemann Explore Science contains a wide range of ideas for interaction that includes things to do, questions to ask and resources to support learning. Your professional role is in the effective deployment of those resources.

The Heinemann Explore Science website

This provides a full range of editable planning materials, generic writing frames and presentation templates to support students in recording and presenting their work.

The website also provides digital e-book versions of all the *Readers* for each Grade and for the *Student Books* and *Workbooks*, so that worksheets can be downloaded and printed if needed.

Using ICT for research

Students should develop their research skills using a variety of secondary sources. Throughout the *Student Book*, students are given opportunities to use ICT to research the answers to questions related to the topic of the lesson. At the end of each Unit, a more open question with reference only to the appropriate area of study is introduced to encourage students to develop search skills and strategies.

The Heinemann Explore Science Readers

These have been written bearing in mind the language needs of students for whom English is not a first language. Each book complements a Unit in the scheme. They offer interesting illustrations and simple, engaging text. Word count increases with higher Grades. They can be used as individual readers, books to read at home, or for group reading. They can be used for vocabulary and language exercise, and there are suggestions for activities at the back of each book – from crosswords to team games.

Used alongside the other components of the scheme, they offer opportunities for developing science and language, hand in hand.

Health and safety issues

Primary science is a very safe activity, but that does not mean that you should not consider health and safety issues when you plan, or that you should feel unsupported, either. *Heinemann Explore Science* highlights specific safety issues in lessons when appropriate, and you should also engage in your own risk assessment and take appropriate precautions. This should not be demanding; it involves looking at your students, your circumstances and support staff, and ensuring that you have noted, minimized and if necessary recorded any apparent hazards. It is essential to share this risk assessment with other adults in the classroom.

Every adult on the school site should be familiar with the school's Health and Safety Policy, and especially how it reflects on their responsibilities. They should know the location and proper use of safety equipment. All adults have a responsibility for their own safety, and that of their students in school, whatever their age. This is a responsibility you share with others. Teaching assistants, for example, are often responsible for small groups of students doing practical activities – their supervision may be vital where a hazard has been recognized, for example, when using a cooker. Working with a small group like this offers opportunities not just for realistic but negative teaching ('Don't touch that – it's hot!') but also for positive modelling of safe behaviour ('Now how should I pick this up?').

You can give a very positive image of health and safety issues by performing a routine risk assessment while planning an activity, and encouraging students to make their own assessment of risk, and take their own precautions. Engaging students in safety planning helps them to understand the importance of not taking risks. If students are simply told what is safe without explanation they are less likely to take it as seriously as when they are themselves involved in safety planning.

Here are a few general common-sense reminders:

Food: Eating and drinking is forbidden in school science labs, but some of primary science is concerned with food – science activities may require students to eat, but only with your permission. Fingers do get sucked, and foods are tempting. Ensure that guidelines on 'what to eat' are clear and take into account ethnicity, custom, parental wishes and allergies.

Present the best practice in food handling: the cleaning and/or covering of tables, and the use of cooking utensils kept only for this purpose. Pupils should know not to enter the food area unless they are in the practical group (mark or point out an area that can only be entered with clean hands and wearing an apron). Protective clothing not only keeps the students' clothes clean but also prevents food contamination. It should be kept solely for food use. PVC aprons or smocks (coveralls) can be cleaned by wiping with an antibacterial cleaner. Pull-on sleeves can be worn with aprons. Washable aprons should be hot washed at least once a term.

Laminated plastic tables are ideal. Wooden tables (or damaged laminated tables) should be covered with clean plastic tablecloths kept specifically for food. Older students can use antibacterial cleaners after an initial thorough clean by an adult. Spray or wipe all food preparation surfaces including chopping boards with the antibacterial cleaner, wipe with a clean cloth and leave to dry before using.

Nobody – pupil or adult – should work with food if they are unwell, including sickness, diarrhoea, colds, coughs and other infections. Cuts must be covered with a clean waterproof dressing – blue plasters show up if they drop into food! Supervise students washing hands before food work, or after using the toilet. Provide colourless, perfume-free liquid soap and running water. If a hot air dryer is not available, provide disposable paper towels or paper roller towels. Discourage students from touching their face, hair or other parts of their body, and from coughing or sneezing over food.

Electricity: Teach students about the dangers of mains electricity. Students live with electricity and refusing them experience of it is comparable to not teaching them road safety rules for fear of traffic accidents. Mains electricity has a far greater 'push' round the circuit than battery electricity. It is this greater push that kills. The human body is not a good conductor of electricity, but it conducts electricity far better when wet. Work with low-voltage 'battery' electricity is not risky.

Forces: Many activities in science (and technology) put students at risk because little thought is given to possible outcomes. What will happen if the elastic band snaps, the bag breaks, or the liquid spills? Students may take unnecessary risks too, by not using basic science equipment (eye protection, a cutting board or bench hook) that could keep them safe. Testing-to-breaking-point activities in topics such as Forces can be dangerous unless students have considered the consequences of breakage. Wearing well-fitting eye protection when appropriate, and keeping hands and feet out of the way are important. So is considering where you will fall if you are applying effort to an activity.

Animals: The key factor is the welfare of both students and animals. The learning outcome is an understanding of animal welfare and a positive educational experience of (say) a small mammal. It's important to ensure that none of the students has an allergy to animal fur. If you introduce family pets, it's unlikely that they are used to being surrounded by a group of excited students.

Introduce any animal to a group/class yourself. Talk about them, drawing out what the students know, and what they think about how the animal might behave. Students empathize with small animals, and will understand that they could be easily frightened. You might draw out questions they would like to ask about them. Set up a table with you or a prepared, supporting adult in charge. Small groups go to the table in turn, washing their hands thoroughly, under supervision, in advance.

The adult should handle the animal throughout the group activity. Students could ask their questions first, and then take it in turns to stroke the animal at the end, which reduces the chances that students will go rubbing their eyes or sucking their fingers afterwards! Stroking the back of a mammal's head is a useful lesson in how to calm an animal. After their experience, they should wash their hands again, under supervision.

General advice: Younger students can be expected to be able to control risks to themselves and others. They commonly know what is dangerous. Classroom accidents are frequently the result of students forgetting what is sensible because they are caught up in an activity, especially if it is exciting science!

Essential safety advice is contained in a book from the Association for Science Education called *'Be Safe!'* and every teacher should be aware of it and its contents. *Be Safe!* is available from The Association for Science Education, College Lane, Hatfield, Herts. AL10 9AA, UK

info@ase.org.uk website: www.ase.org.uk *Be Safe!* ISBN: 978 0 86357 426 9

Schools from around the world are members of CLEAPSS, the advisory service for health and safety in science education. CLEAPSS offers informative publications, a staffed helpline, and a members' website. It is an essential source of science safety knowledge.

CLEAPSS School Science Service

www.cleapss.org.uk

Curriculum structure of *Heinemann Explore Science*

Heinemann Explore Science has been very carefully structured to ensure a progressive development in the students using the course, both of scientific process skills and also of knowledge and understanding. This complements the approach taken in the Cambridge Primary Science Curriculum Framework (2011).

The development of scientific process skills throughout the complete course is shown in this skills ladder:

Heinemann Explore Science Science Skills Ladder

Skills Domain	Year 1 Children have opportunities:	Year 2 Children have opportunities:	Year 3 Children have opportunities:	Year 4 Children have opportunities:	Year 5 Children have opportunities:	Year 6 Children have opportunities:
1. **Ideas and evidence in science**	to collect evidence to try to answer a question	to collect evidence to try to answer a question	to collect evidence in a variety of contexts to answer a question or test an idea	to collect evidence in a variety of contexts to test an idea or prediction based on their scientific knowledge and understanding	to consider how scientists have combined evidence from observation and measurement with creative thinking to suggest new ideas and explanations for phenomena	to consider how scientists have combined evidence from observation and measurement with creative thinking to suggest new ideas and explanations for phenomena
2. **Investigative skills** **Planning investigative work**	to test ideas suggested to them and say what they think will happen	to suggest some ideas and questions based on simple knowledge and say how they might find out about them; to say what they think might happen; and to think about and discuss whether comparisons and tests are fair or unfair	in a variety of contexts, to suggest questions and ideas and how to test them; to make predictions about what will happen; to think about how to collect sufficient evidence in some contexts; and to consider what makes a test unfair or evidence sufficient and, with help, plan fair tests	to suggest questions that can be tested and make predictions about what will happen, some of which are based on scientific knowledge; to design a fair test or plan how to collect sufficient evidence; and, in some contexts, to choose what apparatus to use and what to measure	to make predictions of what will happen based on scientific knowledge and understanding, and suggest how to test these; to use knowledge and understanding to plan how to carry out a fair test or how to collect sufficient evidence to test an idea; and to identify factors that need to be taken into consideration in different contexts	to decide how to turn ideas into a form that can be tested and, where appropriate, to make predictions using scientific knowledge and understanding; to identify factors that are relevant to a particular situation; to choose what evidence to collect to investigate a question, ensuring the evidence is sufficient; and to choose what equipment to use

Heinemann Explore Science Science Skills Ladder

Skills Domain	Year 1 Children have opportunities:	Year 2 Children have opportunities:	Year 3 Children have opportunities:	Year 4 Children have opportunities:	Year 5 Children have opportunities:	Year 6 Children have opportunities:
3. **Obtaining and presenting evidence**		to make observations using appropriate senses; to make some measurements of length using standard and non-standard measures; and to present some findings in simple tables and block graphs	to make observations and comparisons; to measure length, volume of liquid and time in standard measures using simple measuring equipment effectively; and to present results in drawing, bar charts and tables	to make observations and comparisons of relevant features in a variety of contexts; to make measurements of temperature, time and force as well as measurements of length; to begin to think about why measurements of length should be repeated; and to present results in bar charts and tables	to make relevant observations; to consolidate measurement of volume, temperature, time and length; to measure pulse rate; to think about why observations and measurements should be repeated; and to present results in bar charts and line graphs	to make a variety of relevant observations and measurements using simple apparatus correctly; to decide when observations and measurements need to be checked, by repeating, to give more reliable data; and to use tables, bar charts and line graphs to present results
4. **Considering evidence and approach**	to communicate observations orally, in drawing, by labelling and in simple writing; to make simple comparisons and groupings that relate to differences and similarities between living things and objects; in some cases to say what their observations show, and whether it was what they expected; and to draw simple conclusions and explain what they did	to make simple comparisons, identifying similarities and differences between living things, objects and events; to say what results show; to say whether their predictions were supported; in some cases to use knowledge to explain what was found out and to draw conclusions; and to explain what they did	to draw conclusions from results and begin to use scientific knowledge to suggest explanations for them; and to make generalizations and begin to identify simple patterns in results presented in tables	to identify simple trends and patterns in results presented in tables, charts and graphs and to suggest explanations for some of these; to explain what the evidence shows and whether it supports any predictions made; and to link the evidence to scientific knowledge and understanding in some contexts	to decide whether results support any prediction; to begin to evaluate repeated results; to recognize and make predictions from patterns in data and suggest explanations for these using scientific knowledge and understanding; to interpret data and think about whether it is sufficient to draw conclusions; and to draw conclusions indicating whether these match any prediction made	to make comparisons; to evaluate repeated results; to identify patterns in results and results that do not appear to fit the pattern; to use results to draw conclusions and to make further predictions; to suggest and evaluate explanations for these predictions using scientific knowledge and understanding; and to say whether the evidence supports any prediction made

Heinemann Explore Science Curriculum Matching Chart for Grade 6

This chart shows where all of the topics and Learning Objectives specified in the Cambridge Primary Science Curriculum Framework (2011) are covered in the *Heinemann Explore Science* course.

Learning Objectives	*Student Book* coverage	Supporting coverage in *Teacher's Book* or *Workbook*
Scientific enquiry		
Scientific enquiry: Ideas and evidence		
Consider how scientists have combined evidence from observation and measurement with creative thinking to suggest new ideas and explanations for phenomena.	Unit 2: Scientists • Alhazen and how we see pp.22–3 • Brunel and the railways pp.24–5 • You are a scientist pp.26–7	*Teacher's Book* 6, pp.40–49 *Workbook* 6, p.12
Collect evidence and data to test ideas including predictions.	Unit 1: Interdependence and adaptation • Feeding plants pp.4–5 Unit 4: More about dissolving • Dissolving jelly pp.48–9 • Dissolving sugar pp.50–1 • Mixing solids and liquids pp.52–3 Unit 5: Reversible and irreversible changes • Making new materials pp.58–9 • Irreversible change pp.60–1	*Teacher's Book* 6, pp.16–39 *Teacher's Book* 6, pp.64–79 *Teacher's Book* 6, pp.80–89 *Workbook* 6, p.5
Scientific enquiry: Plan investigative work		
Discuss how to turn ideas into a form that can be tested.	Unit 1: Interdependence and adaptation • Feeding plants pp.4–5 • What a load of rubbish! pp.18–19 Unit 4: More about dissolving • Dissolving jelly pp.48–9 • Dissolving sugar pp.50–1 • Mixing solids and liquids 52–3 Unit 6: Forces in action • Investigating upthrut pp.70–1 • Stretching springs pp.72–3 • Investigating aeroplanes pp.76–7 Unit 8: Enquiry in context • Thinking like a scientist pp.94–5	*Teacher's Book* 6, pp.16–39 *Teacher's Book* 6, pp.64–79 *Teacher's Book* 6, pp.90–107 *Teacher's Book* 6, pp.120–129
Make predictions using scientific knowledge and understanding.	Unit 4: More about dissolving • Dissolving jelly pp.48–9 • Dissolving sugar pp.50–1 • Mixing solids and liquids pp.52–3	*Teacher's Book* 6, pp.64–79
Choose what evidence to collect to investigate a question, ensuring that the evidence is sufficient.	Unit 1: Interdependence and adaptation • Feeding plants pp.4–5 • Identifying living things pp.6–7 • Food chains pp.8–9 Unit 2: Scientists • You are a scientist pp.26–7 Unit 4: More about dissolving • Dissolving jelly pp.48–9 • Dissolving sugar pp.50–1 Unit 6: Forces in action • Investigating upthrust pp.70–1 • Investigating aeroplanes pp.76–7	*Teacher's Book* 6, pp.16–39 *Teacher's Book* 6, pp.40–49 *Teacher's Book* 6, pp.64–79 *Teacher's Book* 6, pp.90–107
Identify factors that are relevant to a particular situation.	Unit 1: Interdependence and adaptation • Identifying living things pp.6–7 • Life in the soil pp.12–13 Unit 2: Scientists • You are a scientist pp.26–7 Unit 6: Forces in action • Direction of forces pp.68–9 • Investigating upthrust pp.70–1	*Teacher's Book* 6, pp.16–39 *Teacher's Book* 6, pp.40–49 *Teacher's Book* 6, pp.90–107
Choose which equipment to use.	Unit 1: Interdependence and adaptation • Healthy plants pp.2–3 • Feeding plants pp.4–5	*Teacher's Book* 6, pp.16–39

	Unit 4: More about dissolving • Dissolving jelly pp.48–9 • Dissolving sugar pp.50–1	*Teacher's Book* 6, pp.64–79
	Unit 5: Reversible and irreversible changes • Making new materials pp.58–9 • Irreversible change pp.60–1	*Teacher's Book* 6, pp.80–89
	Unit 6: Forces in action • Investigating upthrust pp.70–1 • Stretching springs pp.72–3 • Investigating aeroplanes pp.76–7	*Teacher's Book* 6, pp.90–107
	Unit 7: Changing circuits • Testing wires pp.82–3	*Teacher's Book* 6, pp.108–119
	Unit 8: Enquiry in context • Common cars pp.90–1 • Burglar alarms pp.92–3	*Teacher's Book* 6, pp.120–129 *Workbook* 6, p.21

Scientific enquiry: Obtain and present evidence

Make a variety of relevant observations and measurements using simple apparatus correctly.	Unit 1: Interdependence and adaptation • Feeding plants pp.4–5	*Teacher's Book* 6, pp.16–39
	Unit 4: More about dissolving • Dissolving jelly pp.48–9 • Dissolving sugar pp.50–1 • Mixing solids and liquids pp.52–3	*Teacher's Book* 6, pp.64–79
	Unit 5: Reversible and irreversible changes • Making new materials pp.58–9 • Irreversible change pp.60–1	*Teacher's Book* 6, pp.80–89
	Unit 6: Forces in action • Investigating upthrust pp.70–1 • Stretching springs pp.72–3 • Investigating aeroplanes pp.76–7	*Teacher's Book* 6, pp.90–106
	Unit 7: Changing circuits • Testing wires pp.82–3	*Teacher's Book* 6, pp.108–119
	Unit 8: Enquiry in context • Thinking like a scientist pp.94–5	*Teacher's Book* 6, pp.120–129
Decide when observations and measurements need to be checked by repeating to give more reliable data.	Unit 1: Interdependence and adaptation • Feeding plants pp.4–5	*Teacher's Book* 6, pp.16–39
	Unit 2: Scientists • You are a scientist pp.26–7	*Teacher's Book* 6, pp.40–49
	Unit 4: More about dissolving • Dissolving jelly pp.48–9 • Dissolving sugar pp.50–1	*Teacher's Book* 6, pp.64–79
	Unit 6: Forces in action • Investigating upthrust pp.70–1 • Investigating aeroplanes pp.76–7	*Teacher's Book* 6, pp.90–106
Use tables, bar charts and line graphs to present results.	Unit 1: Interdependence and adaptation • Healthy plants pp.2–3 • Feeding plants pp.4–5 • Plant producer pp.10–11	*Teacher's Book* 6, pp.16–39
	Unit 2: Scientists • Brunel and the railways pp.24–5	*Teacher's Book* 6, pp.40–49
	Unit 4: More about dissolving • Dissolving jelly pp.48–9 • Dissolving sugar pp.50–15 • Mixing solids and liquids pp.52–3	*Teacher's Book* 6, pp.64–79 *Workbook* 6, p.28
	Unit 5: Reversible and irreversible changes • Making new materials pp.58–9 • Irreversible change pp.60–1	*Teacher's Book* 6, pp.80–89
	Unit 6: Forces in action • Investigating upthrust pp.70–1 • Stretching springs pp.72–3 • Investigating aeroplanes pp.76–7	*Teacher's Book* 6, pp.90–107
	Unit 7: Changing circuits • Testing wires pp.82–3	*Teacher's Book* 6, pp.108–119
	Unit 8: Enquiry in context • Common cars pp.90–1 • Burglar alarms pp.92–3 • Thinking like a scientist pp.94–5	*Teacher's Book* 6, pp.120–129 *Workbook* 6, p.5

Scientific enquiry: Consider evidence and approach

Make comparisons.	Unit 1: Interdependence and adaptation • Adapting to a habitat pp.14–15 Unit 3: Humans • Where are your organs? pp.30–1 Unit 8: Enquiry in context • Common cars pp.90–1 • Burglar alarms pp.92–3 • Thinking like a scientists pp.94–5	*Teacher's Book* 6, pp.16–39 *Teacher's Book* 6, pp.50–63 *Teacher's Book* 6, pp.120–129
Evaluate repeated results.	Unit 4: More about dissolving • Dissolving sugar pp.50–1 Unit 6: Forces in action • Investigating upthrust pp.70–1 • Investigating aeroplanes pp.76–7	*Teacher's Book* 6, pp.64–79 *Teacher's Book* 6, pp.90–107
Identify patterns in results and results that do not appear to fit the pattern.	Unit 1: Interdependence and adaptation • Plant producer pp.10–11 Unit 4: More about dissolving • Dissolving sugar pp.50–1 Unit 6: Forces in action • Investigating upthrust pp.70–1 • Stretching springs pp.72–3 Unit 8: Enquiry in context • Common cars pp.90–1	*Teacher's Book* 6, pp.16–39 *Teacher's Book* 6, pp.64–79 *Teacher's Book* 6, pp.90–107 *Teacher's Book* 6, pp.120–129 *Workbook* 6, pp.5, 65
Use results to draw conclusions and to make further predictions.	Unit 1: Interdependence and adaptation • Feeding plants pp.4–5	*Teacher's Book* 6, pp.16–39 *Workbook* 6, pp.8, 28
Suggest and evaluate explanations for predictions using scientific knowledge and understanding and communicate these clearly to others.	Unit 1: Interdependence and adaptation • Feeding plants pp.4–5 • Being responsible pp.16–17 Unit 4: More about dissolving • Dissolving jelly pp.48–9 • Mixing solids and liquids pp.52–3 Unit 6: Forces in action • Investigating upthrust pp.70–1 Unit 8: Enquiry in context • Burglar alarms pp.92–3 • Thinking like a scientist pp.94–5	*Teacher's Book* 6, pp.16–39 *Teacher's Book* 6, pp.64–79 *Teacher's Book* 6, pp.90–107 *Teacher's Book* 6, pp.120–129 *Workbook* 6, p.8
Say if and how evidence supports any prediction made.	Unit 1: Interdependence and adaptation • Feeding plants pp.4–5 Unit 2: Scientists • Alhazen and how we see pp.22–23 Unit 4: More about dissolving • Dissolving sugar pp.50–51 Unit 5: Reversible and irreversible changes • Making new materials pp.58–59 Unit 6: Forces in action • Investigating upthrust pp.63, 70–71	*Teacher's Book* 6, pp.22–23 *Workbook* 6, p.5 *Teacher's Book* 6, pp.42–43 *Teacher's Book* 6, pp.74–75 *Workbook* 6, p.24 *Teacher's Book* 6, pp.84–85 *Workbook* 6, p.34 *Teacher's Book* 6, pp.98–99 *Workbook* 6, p.39, 49

Biology

Biology: Humans and animals

Use scientific names for some major organs of body systems.	Unit 3: Humans • Where are your organs? pp.30–1	*Teacher's Book* 6, pp.50–63 *Workbook* 6, p.9
Identify the position of major organs in the body.	Unit 3: Humans • Where are your organs? pp.30–1 • Organization pp.32–3 • Digestion pp.34–5 • Breathing in and out pp.36–7	*Teacher's Book* 6, pp.50–63 *Workbook* 6, p.9
Describe the main functions of the major organs of the body.	Unit 3: Humans • Where are your organs? pp.30–1 • Organization pp.32–3 • Digestion 34–5 • Breathing in and out pp.36–7	*Teacher's Book* 6, pp.50–63 *Workbook* 6, pp.9–12
Explain how the functions of the major organs are essential.	Unit 3: Humans • Where are your organs? pp.30–1 • Organization pp.32–3 • Digestion pp.34–5 • Breathing in and out pp.36–7	*Teacher's Book* 6, pp.50–63 *Workbook* 6, pp.10–11

Biology: Living things in the environment

Explore how humans have positive and negative effects on the environment, e.g. loss of species, protection of habitats.	Unit 1: Interdependence and adaptation • Being responsible pp.16–17 • What a load of rubbish! pp.18–19	*Teacher's Book* 6, pp.16–39 *Workbook* 6, pp.2,3

Explore a number of ways of caring for the environment, e.g. recycling, reducing waste, reducing energy consumption, not littering, encouraging others to care for the environment.	Unit 1: Interdependence and adaptation • Being responsible pp.16–17 • What a load of rubbish! pp.18–19	*Teacher's Book* 6, pp.16–39
Know how food chains can be used to represent feeding relationships in a habitat and present these in text and diagrams.	Unit 1: Interdependence and adaptation • Identifying living things pp.6–7 • Food chains pp.8–9	*Teacher's Book* 6, pp.16–39
Know that food chains begin with a plant (the producer), which uses energy from the Sun.	Unit 1: Interdependence and adaptation • Identifying living things pp.6–7	*Teacher's Book* 6, pp.16–39 *Workbook* 6, pp.1,4
Understand the terms *producer, consumer, predator* and *prey*.	Unit 1: Interdependence and adaptation • Identifying living things pp.6–7 • Food chains pp.8–9	*Teacher's Book* 6, pp.16–39
Explore and construct food chains in a particular habitat.	Unit 1: Interdependence and adaptation • Food chains pp.8–9	*Teacher's Book* 6, pp.16–39

Chemistry

Chemistry: Material changes

Distinguish between reversible and irreversible changes.	Unit 5: Reversible and irreversible changes • Separation pp.56–7 • Making new materials pp.58–9 • Irreversible change pp.60–1	*Teacher's Book* 6, pp.80–89 *Workbook* 6, pp.18–20
Explore how solids can be mixed and how it is often possible to separate them again.	Unit 5: Reversible and irreversible changes • Separation pp.56–7 • Making new materials pp.58–9 • Irreversible change pp.60–1	*Teacher's Book* 6, pp.80–89 *Workbook* 6, pp.14,15
Observe, describe, record and begin to explain changes that occur when some solids are added to water.	Unit 5: Reversible and irreversible changes • Separation pp.56–7	*Teacher's Book* 6, pp.80–89
Explore how, when solids do not dissolve or react with water, they can be separated by filtering, which is similar to sieving.	Unit 4: More about dissolving • Filtering and sieving pp.42–3	*Teacher's Book* 6, pp.64–79 *Workbook* 6, p.17
Explore how some solids dissolve in water to form solutions and, although the solid cannot be seen, the substance is still present.	Unit 4: More about dissolving • Separating solids and liquids pp.44–5 • Making water pure pp.46–7	*Teacher's Book* 6, pp.64–79

Physics

Physics: Forces and motion

Distinguish between mass measured in kilograms (kg) and weight measured in newtons, noting that kilograms are used in everyday life.	Unit 6: Forces in action • Weight and gravity pp.64–5	*Teacher's Book* 6, pp.90–107 *Workbook* 6, p.21
Recognize and use units of force, mass and weight and identify the direction in which forces act.	Unit 6: Forces in action • Energy in movement pp.66–7 • Direction of forces pp.68–9	*Teacher's Book* 6, pp.90–107 *Workbook* 6, pp.22,24
Understand the notion of energy in movement.	Unit 6: Forces in action • Energy in movement pp.66–7	*Teacher's Book* 6, pp.90–107
Recognize friction (including air resistance) as a force which can affect the speed at which objects move and which sometimes stops things moving.	Unit 6: Forces in action • Air resistance pp.74–5	*Teacher's Book* 6, pp.90–107 *Workbook* 6, pp.23,25

Physics: Electricity and magnetism

Investigate how some materials are better conductors of electricity than others.	Unit 7: Changing circuits • Exploring conductivity pp.84–5	*Teacher's Book* 6, pp.108–119 *Workbook* 6, p.29
Investigate how some metals are good conductors of electricity while most other materials are not.	Unit 7: Changing circuits • Exploring conductivity pp.84–5	*Teacher's Book* 6, pp.108–119
Know why metals are used for cables and wires and why plastics are used to cover wires and as covers for plugs and switches.	Unit 7: Changing circuits • Exploring conductivity pp.84–5	*Teacher's Book* 6, pp.108–119 *Workbook* 6, p.28
Predict and test the effects of making changes to circuits, including length or thickness of wire and the number and type of components.	Unit 7: Changing circuits • Electrical circuits pp.80–1 • Testing wires pp.82–3	*Teacher's Book* 6, pp.108–119 *Workbook* 6, p.30
Represent series circuits with drawings and conventional symbols.	Unit 7: Changing circuits • Electrical circuits pp.80–1	*Teacher's Book* 6, pp.108–119 *Workbook* 6, pp.26,27

Resources for *Heinemann Explore Science* Grade 6

Science equipment and durable items

balance scale
cold-water paste
digital balance
digital camera or a video camera
  with a timer
digital microscope
floor vinyl
forcemeter
hand lens or magnifying glass
light sensor
magnetic and non-magnetic
  metals
magnets
masses, up to and including 500 g
measuring jug or cylinder

measuring stick or tape measure
metal samples
metre ruler
models of teeth or real teeth
  (milk and adult)
newtonmeter
OHP transparencies
pH indicator strips
plank or ramp
rocks and minerals reference
  books and field guides
sieves with different-sized holes
simple watering systems, e.g.
  use film canisters to measure
  watering

small beakers or glasses
small mirrors
spinner template
stopwatch or other seconds timer
strips of metal
strips of plastic
strips of wood
video camera
weighing scales
whiteboard
wooden block and pieces of wood

Consumables and items locally available

backing/display paper
beads with large holes
blotting paper
bricks (to support end of a plank)
bubble wrap
card
cardboard
carpet
carrier bags
chocolate
clay
clear glass jars
cork
cotton reels
cotton wool
cress seeds
different soils or sand, clay, peat
  and compost mixtures
disclosing tablets
dog food and hamster mix
  (including tins, pictures, etc.)
elastic bands
examples of all the food groups as
  pictures
felt
filter paper
fizzy drinks

foil
food colouring
funnels or the tops of pop bottles
graph paper
hoops
ink
J-cloth
kitchen scales (operated with a
  spring)
knives
leather bags
liquid soap
long tube or plastic pop bottle
  with the top cut off
marbles or small masses (e.g.
  coins)
matchsticks
mouthwash
paper bags
paper clips
paper towel
permanent marker pen
pictures of different plants
plastic bags
plastic tub
Plasticine
plates

pop bottles
pot plants
rocks
sand
sandpaper
saucers
skulls or diagrams of different
  animals
small plant pots
socks in different thicknesses,
  colours and sizes
soft cloth
spoons
steel paper clips
sticky tape
string
sweet jars
tea-stained mugs
toothbrushes
toothpaste
toy cars
turfs of grass
variety of fruit and vegetables.
vegetable oil
very small pots
wallpaper paste or clear liquid
  soap

Unit 1: Interdependence and adaptation

The objectives for this Unit are that students should be able to:

- Understand that all living creatures are part of a food chain

- Find out how to keep food chains healthy and unpolluted

- Take part in scientific investigations and decide on the best way to clearly present their results

- Use their scientific background knowledge to predict findings and explain their ideas.

SB p.1 ***Science background***

The poem referred to in the *Student Book* is called *There Was an Old Lady Who Swallowed a Fly*. In the poem, she swallows a fly, then a spider to catch the fly and then a bird to catch the spider.

She eventually swallows a cat to catch the bird, a dog to catch the cat, a cow to catch the dog and a horse, after which she's dead – not surprisingly! The old lady knows that different animals eat each other and was using this to try to catch the fly she accidentally swallowed.

All living things are interlinked by the need for energy to live and grow. Some animals eat other animals, e.g. a fox eats a hare. If there weren't any hares, then the foxes would suffer; if there were lots, there would be more foxes. Some animals eat plants for energy, e.g. grass provides the food for the hare. The more grass there is the greater the number of hares. Plants get something out of this too. The faeces that animals leave on the ground help to provide plants with the nutrients they need to grow well. These are the same nutrients that farmers will replace with fertilizers if they keep animals off the ground where they grow crops. Farmers sometimes spread manure over their fields. If plants grow in the same place all the time, they use up all the nutrients in the soil. These nutrients need to be replaced, with fertilizers or manure. If nothing is added to the soil, the plants may still grow, because rainwater carries some nutrients.

If an organism changes to benefit from its habitat this is called adaptation. Birds have developed beaks that are the best shape to eat the food available in their habitats. Fish have developed gills to breathe underwater and tails to swim faster. Hares have developed long ears to hear foxes coming, and strong muscles to run away fast. Animal and plant structure is a result of adaptation.

Language	
Adapted	Changed in some way to suit the surroundings, or habitat.
Consumer	Any organism that eats another – all animals are consumers.
Environment	The world and the place that is surrounding us or an organism.
Fertilizer	A mixture of chemicals given to plants to help them grow.
Food chain	A list of organisms, with arrows to show how the energy moves from the plant to the animals. Most are very short. They may be presented as a cycle – the animal waste and even its dead body return to the soil to fertilize plants.
Fossil fuel	Produced from organisms that died millions of years ago, e.g. oil from microbes in the oceans (petrol and diesel) and coal from decaying plant material in swamps (used in power stations to generate electricity).
Key	A step-by-step system used to identify an organism.

Nutrient	Special chemical requirement.
Organism	An individual living thing.
Pollution	Any unwanted or undesirable change to the environment, normally caused by humans, anything from dropping litter, to burning fossil fuels and releasing carbon dioxide into the atmosphere.
Predator	An animal that eats another animal.
Prey	An organism eaten by another one, usually an animal, although some plants are carnivorous, e.g. the Venus fly trap.
Producer	A green plant, so called because it uses energy from sunlight to produce food.
Reduce	Cut down on the amount that we use, i.e. not buying so much.
Reuse	Using cardboard, plastics etc. for a different purpose or even the same purpose, rather than throwing away into landfill or dump sites. It is also linked to upgrading rather than throwing away and purchasing new.
Recycle	Reuse of objects and materials. For example, glass can be recycled indefinitely.

Ideas for reducing the amount of waste humans make are often grouped together as Reduce, Reuse, Recycle and recover. Recover refers to the practice of putting waste products to use. For example, decomposing garbage produces methane gas, one of the greenhouse gases, which some landfill sites recover and burn for energy rather than letting it dissipate.

Species	A group of organisms with similar characteristics, e.g. wolves, humans, cats etc.

The Words to learn list on page 1 of the *Student Book* can be used to make a classroom display.

Resources

- *Living Things in Their Enviroment* Reader
- Plants that have been kept in the dark, to show very pale or yellow leaves. Try covering some grass with black polythene or a carpet tile
- Tomato plants or other plants kept in various conditions, e.g. no light, little water, poor soil, no feed, as well as healthy ones
- Peace lilies or day lilies if possible
- Hand lenses or magnifying glasses
- Containers, e.g. matchboxes or insect viewers, to hold and collect organisms
- Soil samples
- Sheets or pots of gel that can be obtained from garden centres or school suppliers. They allow you to see when a plant cutting has rooted
- Hormone rooting powder and some transparent containers
- Packets, sachets and bottles of plant feeds and fertilizers, e.g. Baby Bio, tomato feed, lawn feed, etc.
- A range of vegetables for identification, including some that students might not know
- Empty vitamin and mineral bottles, e.g. multi-vitamins and single or joint ones
- A variety of labels for indoor and outdoor plants.

⚠ Ensure that students to do not touch the contents of the fertilizer containers. Use empty and washed out containers for the data handling exercise. For the enquiry, you or another member of staff will need to dispense and supervise the use of fertilizers.

Bright ideas

If you don't have access to different soil types, use compost or normal garden soil with soil materials added, e.g. pebbles, leaf litter, or some clay or sand.

Collect soils from different gardens spread over a wide area, to ensure variety. Make sure you collect a large bag full and label its source; this can be used for future years! There may be soil samples left from the investigation in Grade 3.

Skills check

Students need to:

- predict what will happen
- make careful observations
- decide on the most appropriate way to present results to aid explanation
- use their background knowledge to explain their results
- use a range of secondary sources to research
- say if their evidence matches their prediction.

Some students will:

- know that green plants are a source of food for animals
- recognize that plants need sunlight, air and water to produce new material for growth.

Knowledge check

- Students should be familiar with what a habitat is.
- Students should understand that some living things eat one another.
- Students should know what plants need in order to grow well.

Links to other subjects

Literacy:	Reading and following simple instructions, e.g. those for growing plants. Researching and summarizing from a range of other sources.
Numeracy:	Organizing and interpreting simple data in tables, e.g. recording the growth of plants.
Information Communication Technology (ICT):	Using a light sensor connected to a computer. Using PowerPoint to produce a presentation. Using the Internet to research. Using a graphing program.
Personal Social Health Education (PSHE):	Recognizing the need to protect the environment, e.g. Knowing that depleting soil affects plant growth, and the impact of humans upon the enviroment.

Let's find out...

The Unit opens with this question:

*Farmers want plants to grow well. They give the plants **nutrients**, called **fertilizers**. When it rains, some fertilizer gets washed into rivers and streams. Is this a problem for the animals that live there? Would any animals gain? How?*

*Farmers put **pesticides** on their crops. What does a pesticide do? They also get into rivers and streams. Is this good or bad? Why?*

Discuss the problem. Students may be aware of farmers spreading manure on fields to help the plants grow. The topic will give them information on how the fertilizers provide the nutrients for better plant growth. Pesticides kill pests – the 'cide' means 'to kill'. There is also herbicide (to kill plants) and insecticide (to kill insects).

Unit 1: Interdependence and adaptation – Healthy plants

The objectives for this lesson are that students should be able to:

- Understand what plants use light for

- Discover why fertilizers are added to soil

- Investigate whether plants can grow without soil

- Carry out a scientific investigation and explain their results.

Starter
SB pp.2–3

- How can plants be grown in the desert? Explain that watering the desert can make it fertile. Most soils contain the tiny amounts of minerals and other trace elements that plants need to grow and be healthy.

- Show the students any grass outside that has been kept under polythene. Ask if the grass will recover. How can it go green again?

Explain
WS 1

Are you a good gardener?

If you have a plant that hasn't been watered and one that has been lacking sunlight these will allow the students to observe an unhealthy plant and test out their theories more closely, e.g. touching the soil to see if it is moist or not. Make sure the plants aren't actually dead. A pot of wilted basil is ideal to demonstrate lack of water, as it will perk up within an hour of watering. Any plant that should be kept in bright light will suffer most and recover quickest when briefly deprived of light, for example geraniums, which also fail to flower without lots of sunlight. Alternatively, use a plant that will only have its flowers open in daylight, e.g. day lilies.

Bring me sunshine

At this level students do not need to know about photosynthesis in detail.

Plants take in oxygen for respiration as well as using carbon dioxide for photosynthesis but they produce more oxygen than they use. Plants are self-sustaining, but animals are not. Animals need plants to produce oxygen, which is essential to their survival.

Sunlight is a form of energy and this is used to convert water and carbon dioxide into sugars, and then into starch, the stored food of the plant. When we eat a plant, we gain that energy.

Students can use WS 1 to revise the parts of a plant and then answer questions about what each part does.

Things to do
WS 2

Minerals and plant growth

The students will need to look at the ingredients labels of various containers that have held fertilizer or plant food, e.g. plant growth enhancers, tomato feed, etc. Stress that this isn't a plant 'food', but a supplement for the plant, to ensure really good growth. It is similar to humans taking vitamins in their diet.

> ⚠ The containers will need to be clean and students should not touch fertilizer. Wash hands after handling the containers.

Support

Some students will have difficulty with the names of the ingredients in fertilizers. Try asking them to find certain words in the ingredients, e.g. potassium, calcium, magnesium, phosphate or phosphorus, and then tick them off in a table.

Extend

Most students should know that plants need essential nutrients. Some students will recognize that different plants need different nutrients or even different amounts of the same nutrients. More able students can produce a table and bar chart of the amounts of nutrients in fertilizers. Alternatively the students can complete the graph on WS 2 and answer the questions about adding different amounts of fertilizer to a field of corn.

Record

The students' table will provide a record that plants have needs other than water, light and warmth.

Dig deeper

The students should find out that most photosynthesis takes place in the leaf, specifically the upper surface.

Did you know?

The first fact shows students that a plant gives out oxygen as it photosynthesizes and that animals consume the oxygen.

I wonder...

A tomato plant has specific requirements as it has a short growing season and will produce lots of fruits during this time. It grows better with extra nutrients and tomato fertilizer provides these. Plant food for houseplants is intended for feeding plants that need fewer nutrients in total. So the tomatoes will grow, but will do less well if you give them houseplant food rather than tomato fertilizer.

Other ideas

Sunbathers

Measure two leaves on a plant that has been on a sunny windowsill. Cut out three shapes in a piece of foil or card, making sure they aren't bigger than the leaves you've measured. Use a paper clip to carefully hold one shape over the top surface of the leaf and attach the other shape to the bottom surface of another leaf. Attach another piece to a part of the stem. Leave the plant in a sunny place for a week and ask students to explain what happens to the parts you have covered, compared to the rest of the plant. When photosynthesis does not occur then chlorophyll, the green pigment that makes leaves green and also makes food for the plant, is not produced.

Safe fertilizer

Ask the students to design a container to dispense fertilizer without having to touch it. For example, a container with a cap to pour the fertilizer into, or a siphon tube connected to a reservoir to ensure that the correct amount of liquid is dispensed. The fertilizer could be in the form of a tablet, or even a device put in the soil with the plant that allows the liquid food to be slowly released into the pot.

Presentation

Ask the students to create an advert to sell a new plant nutrient. It should be tailored to fit the plant and the person who would be buying it, e.g. tomato fertilizer to gardeners, or houseplant fertilizer to home owners, or food for apple trees to juice makers, etc. These could be filmed for display during an open evening, or the students could create a wall display showing the features they picked up on. The students could use PowerPoint to show how well the plant will grow with and without feeding, by running one photograph on top of another and then speeding it up. Photographs could be taken, with a digital camera, of plants they have grown themselves.

At home

Ask students to look at the labels on plants at home, or in garden centres. What sorts of instructions are written on them? Why?

Plenary

WS 3

Show the students an unhealthy-looking tomato plant if possible which has yellow leaves and isn't very tall. Show that it is in a small pot that doesn't hold a lot of soil. Ask the students what they think is wrong with it, and how they would look after it. They should be able to tell you that it needs some light, some water and a food that suits it, e.g. tomato feed, as this will give the plant the required nutrients.

Alternatively, students can complete WS 3 by giving ways in which Kamil can restore the health of his plants.

Unit 1: Interdependence and adaptation – Feeding plants

The objectives for this lesson are that students should be able to:

- Discover whether a plant needs nutrients added to its diet

- Say if the evidence supports their predictions

- Consider how to improve the accuracy of their investigations

- Write a series of instructions for growing and caring for plants.

SB pp.4–5 — Starter

- Ensure that students understand what happens when seeds germinate – and in what order. *Do the roots grow first?* (Yes.) *Why does the plant need water to grow? Where is the food store for the first growth?* (In the seed.) Some plants, like beans, lift the first 'seed leaves' out of the ground, and they become functional leaves.

- Show some unhealthy and healthy seedlings and discuss the things that could be wrong. Ask students what might happen if they go straight ahead and try any remedy on the unhealthy plant. It might die if the wrong remedy is tried. This is the reason they need to test out their theories before they use them.

The challenge

Read the What to do and speech bubbles on page 4 in the *Student Book*. The challenge is to help farmer Yousef to make all his tomato plants as healthy as each other. This has to be done in a scientific way, by testing ideas before using them. The sick plants have plenty of light and water, as they are next to the healthy plants. These are the main requirements for healthy plant growth. The row may be missing essential nutrients that are found in fresh soil (sometimes the soil becomes 'depleted' if lots of crops have grown in it over a long time). Some of these nutrients can be replaced by fertilizer, known as 'tomato feed'. This term can be confusing, as the plant doesn't need 'food'; it makes its own. Care needs to be taken when using the term 'plant food' or 'tomato

feed', which is often on the containers. The tomato feed is really a mixture of vitamins, minerals and other nutrients that support healthy growth. The fertilizer won't actually help the plant unless it provides what the plant is missing in its 'diet'.

What to do

Using healthy tomato seedlings the students should try each of the suggestions that follow, to produce a set of results that will give them information on what the sick plant requires. Three plants will need to be re-potted in new soil. One of these will be given tomato feed. One will be given houseplant food. Three will be left in the original soil. One of these will be given tomato feed, another houseplant food. The third will be given no additional nutrients, and will act as a 'control'. This gives the students a base line from which to judge if their other plants have grown more than the sick one.

The students should be able to suggest 'a small amount' referring to the instructions on the back of the fertilizer packets.

What you need

- a tray of healthy tomato seedlings (about 10 cm tall)

- new soil (compost)

- fertilizer (tomato feed and houseplant food)

- plastic squeeze pipettes

- trowels

- measuring cylinders

- digital camera or video camera

What to check

The students could choose to count how many new leaves are produced, or measure how much the plant grows in height. They will need to record the number of leaves and the height of each plant before they start the investigation. Check that all plants are kept in the same place and that they have the same amount of water added each time they are watered. The four that are having fertilizer (either tomato feed or houseplant food) will need the same amount of fertilizer added each time they are 'fed'.

Support

Explain that you must always measure the same height, perhaps soil surface to plant top.

Extend

All students should be able to recognize that the plants without any fertilizer don't grow as well as the ones with fertilizer. However, too many nutrients can be harmful to a plant so the fertilizer has to be carefully measured out. Students should discover that the tomato plants grow best with tomato feed added.

Some students may like to try various nutrients and observe the effects on the plants. More able students could measure the height of the plant every day (or every two days to allow for weekends) for each remedy and record this in a table.

What did you find?   WS 4

The students could use the table provided on WS 4 to record their measurements. The students should notice the plant will grow if it is given the nutrients it requires. These may be in the soil already. If they are not then the plant may look sickly. All the plants with new soil in the form of compost and with added nutrients should grow well. The control is the plant without new soil or any added nutrients and this grows least well.

Record

Encourage the students to convert their recorded data into a bar chart.

If they do not have their own data, they could use the Go for Green club's data from the *Student Book*.

Present

Ask each group of students to present their findings, perhaps using ICT. They should include their table of results and charts or graphs. Can they tell the story of the charts/graphs and draw conclusions?

The students could use the digital camera stills, or the video camera time-lapse pictures, to show the difference between the plants with everything they need and the sick plant.

Can you do better?   WS 5

Show the students Class 6's results on WS 5. Read through the results together and then ask your students to answer the questions below.

Now predict

Show the class a marrow or squash. They should notice that its flesh contains a lot of water. Ask them where this 'wetness' comes from. Marrows need plenty of watering while they grow. They also need extra nutrients. Show the students a courgette (zucchini) and a marrow next to one another. They are the same vegetable, but one has been grown for longer.

Ask the students to write some simple instructions on growing marrows. These might be 'Water every day with five pints of water. Feed with a fertilizer every other day. Ensure plenty of sunlight every day. Preferably grow in a glasshouse'.

Other ideas

Cut flowers

Sometimes cut flowers come with a small sachet of white powder. What is it for and how does it work? Plan an investigation to find out, e.g. put one flower into tap water and one in water with the contents of the sachet.

ICT ideas

A light sensor could determine exactly how much light the plant had. A moisture sensor will measure the water content of the soil. The results could help determine the optimum light and moisture needed to provide the best growing conditions.

At home   WS 6

Use WS 6 to revise photosynthesis and the small part played by mineral salts.

Plenary

Return to the original challenge of making the unhealthy plant well. What remedy would they use? Why? Would they do any more trials first?

Unit 1: Interdependence and adaptation – Identifying living things

The objectives for this lesson are that students should be able to:

- Use a key to identify plants and animals

- Explore the relationship between animals and plants in a habitat

- Make their own keys to identify living things

- Explain the different elements of a food chain.

SB pp.6–7 | **_Starter_**

- Use different coloured and shaped buttons to show how identification keys work. Start by splitting the buttons into two groups and deciding on the question that separates them. Write this on the board. Continue to split the buttons into smaller and smaller groups, using simple questions with 'yes' or 'no' answers, or questions that have only a limited range of answers, building up a branching key on the board.

- Show pictures of different animals. How could we make a key to identify these animals? What questions do we need to ask? The 'key' to keys is to ensure that the question only has a 'yes' or 'no' answer. Sometimes the 'nesting' of the questions can lead to problems, but using trial and error works.

- Model one that _doesn't_ work on the board, and discuss what is wrong to illustrate that the order of the questions needs to be thought about carefully.

- Give the students pictures of flowers, plants or insects, so they can practise making their own keys.

Explain

Who are you?

This runs on from the Starter activity. The students could be taken into the school grounds to collect some 'specimens' from a particular habitat and then bring them back to the classroom to identify with a key. The students should be careful to return the animals back to the place they were found after the identification. They should not be encouraged to pick plants, but to work with them in situ.

A consumer survey

The students could be asked to point out the predator and prey in the food chain as well as the producer and the consumers. Remind students that a plant uses air, water and sunlight to make food for growth. Animals eat this food. Although this is not part of the primary curriculum, an accurate definition of a food chain is that it shows the energy from the Sun passing up the food chain to the top predator. This is why the arrows point the way they do, e.g. the arrow moves from the plant to the hare to the fox, showing energy movement, rather than the fox eating the hare and the hare eating the plant. This is a common error that students make when drawing food chains.

Things to do

Are you dependent?

This activity works with a range of animals. A zoo or wildlife park visit is appropriate.

Support

Revisit the habitat discovered earlier in the day and position some pictures or name tags of animals and plants there. Include some that are not part of the habitat and ask the students to pick out the ones that should be found there.

Some students will need help placing arrows the correct way in the food chain. If they place them the wrong way encourage them to see it as the direction in which the food energy moves, UP the food chain from the plant to the top predator.

Extend

All the students should be able to say that the animals depend on the plants for food. All students should be able to recognize the producers and consumers in a habitat.

Some students will know that plants also need animals to distribute their seeds, and that plants provide shelter for animals. They have already learned that we are dependent on plants for renewal of the Earth's atmosphere.

More able students could try to draw food chains from a habitat they have explored. They could try to produce branching and 'go to' keys for other grades to try using them as part of a cross-phase project. They should be able to label some animals as both predators and prey, depending on their place in the food chain.

Record

The students can produce a table of how all the animals and plants depend on each other. They can draw food chains and place the labels on them.

Dig deeper

An ecosystem is the habitat and the community of animals and plants that live there. They are all linked by the food chains within the habitat.

Did you know?

These facts remind students that plants provide the oxygen that all living things need for respiration.

I wonder...

Plants use air, water and sunlight to produce food. They don't need to be able to move around to get these things.

Other ideas

Information cards

The students could make some information cards about the organisms found in their habitat. The information should include: predator or prey or both, eating patterns, consumer or producer, a labelled diagram of the organism, conditions of habitat, e.g. damp, dark, light, warm, etc. The students could also include information on what the organism provides for the habitat and what it requires from it.

Use the cards to play a game like 'Happy Families', collecting all the organisms in a food chain, or all the consumers and all the producers.

An extension of the information cards could be to include the organism's life cycle.

Keys

The students could use a branching key database to produce keys to identify the organisms in the habitat they visited.

Presentation

Encourage students to work in groups to present information about the ecosystem they looked at using PowerPoint. They could discuss what would happen if one of the organisms was removed from the ecosystem.

At home

Ask the students to write one or more food chains for the meal they have that evening. They will need to know the animal their meat or fish comes from and the plant that animal eats. If the students do not eat meat or fish, they should describe what animals eat vegetables or pulses they are eating. It should help to prove that almost all food chains start with a green plant.

Plenary

Show the students a tree leaf and ask them to identify it, using a key. Ask them which tree it is from. Ask how the tree produces its food, and why it is at the start of a food chain. Use the tree as a part of a food chain on the board and ask the students to indicate which is the consumer and which the producer, predator and prey, etc.

Unit 1: Interdependence and adaptation – Food chains

The objectives for this lesson are that students should be able to:

- Construct a food chain for a particular habitat

- Explain how a food chain works and what would happen if it were broken

- Present their food chains as diagrams

- Understand how a collection of food chains are linked by exploring a habitat.

SB pp.8–9 | Starter

- Bring in some processed food: a cheese sandwich for example. Explain that you just picked it on your way to school from a sandwich tree. When the students disagree about that, ask them where they think it came from. *No, not just the shop!* It's made from a number of living things and it's been through quite a process before it got to you.

- Question to develop the 'chain' of events that produced the food, e.g. the bread is made from flour, the flour comes from wheat, which is a plant, which makes its own food from the Sun. The cheese example filling comes from an animal, which eats a plant, which makes its own food from sunlight. You could set this as a challenge for any food to your students.

- Choose an animal in your local environment. *Where does its food come from? Is it food for anything else? So, it eats this; and it's eaten by that. It's a link in a chain really; and we call this a food chain.*

There are a few rare food chains that do not begin with a green plant harnessing the energy of sunlight. In the deepest parts of the sea where light has never penetrated, some bacteria are able to produce energy by breaking down chemicals – this process is called chemosynthesis. But in the vast majority of cases, it's the ability of a green plant to harness the energy of the Sun by photosynthesis that makes a food chain possible. Animals can synthesize some trace requirements; for example, we can produce our own Vitamin D, and some carnivores can synthesize their own Vitamin C.

Explain

A food chain in the sea

Plankton is the name for the microscopic plant and animal life floating in the sea. Green algae in the plankton are able to photosynthesize. They are the base for most marine food chains. Staggering figures are involved: for example, whales will eat millions of krill each day, which in turn have eaten green algae. The green plants are producers and the animals are consumers. The energy flow from the Sun all the way to the top predator is called the food chain. This flow of energy is represented with arrows. An easy way for students to remember the direction of the arrows is to remind them that they point to the stomach of the next consumer.

The energy flows

There are lots of food chains that could be made to match this description. Two are shown. You could ask the students to draw more. This brings in the concept of food webs where a plant or animal can belong in more than one food chain.

Things to do

Draw a food chain

Encourage students to draw a number of food chains including those involving the animals in their immediate habitat. Ensure that the arrows show the flow of energy through the chain from the Sun and the producer to the top predator. Encourage the students, at this stage, to label all the organisms in the chain with the labels of the food chain, e.g. predator, prey, producer, etc. Ask them to explain their food chain to another student to see if it can be drawn accurately from the description. This helps with communication skills.

- Food chains are seldom as simple as this. Many are complicated webs, e.g. both the fish and the whales eat the krill, in the marine food chain. Find out more about food chains in the sea and construct a food web of who eats who. Why do they think it is called a web?

Support

Little should be needed. Most food chains are very short; only three or four links in all.

Extend

Ask students to research more unusual food chains. A good starting point is an animal that eats something unusual. More able students could also start to construct a food web of the sea's organisms from page 8 of the *Student Book*, or from their own habitat. You may need to model this with the marine chains, illustrating why it is called a 'web' (because it has many links and looks a bit like a spider's web!)

Dig deeper

Students should find out more about food chains. They also find out about their own place in food chains and establish that all food webs start in the same way as a food chain – with a producer.

Did you know?

- Scientists investigating volcanoes deep under the Pacific Ocean in 1977 made an amazing discovery. Hot, sulphur-rich water was gushing up from cracks in the seabed. They formed 'black smokers' – mineral chimneys up to ten metres tall that coloured the water black. And these cracks were homes to extraordinary animals. The temperature around these hydrothermal vents can reach 300 degrees Celsius. And living in this hot, sulphurous water were clusters of giant tubeworms up to three metres long. They have no mouth or gut; instead, they live on thick colonies of bacteria growing inside their bodies. The bacteria can use hydrogen sulphide – the chemical that makes bad eggs smell terrible – and methane as energy sources. In exchange for sheltering them, the tubeworms cull the bacteria.

- As the Other ideas on this page will show, breaking a food chain has its effects on the habitat.

I wonder...

Some animals do not move around to find food. For example, barnacles were once famously described as lying on their backs and kicking their food into their mouths. Coral reef creatures are similar to this; they filter out microscopic food from the passing water. But they in turn are eaten by fish with strong jaws that can break open the coral.

Other ideas

Working scientifically

Encourage the students to not only draw food chains, but to describe them in pictures, words and mime to others to see if they can draw them

again with arrows. The discussion could centre around why scientists represent many things with diagrams rather than in paragraphs – because the old adage of a 'picture speaks a thousand words' is true! You could start this by writing up a complicated story of a chain on the board then asking the students to highlight the key words.

Food webs

Few situations are a simple food chain. Most are far more complex and are better described as food webs. You might ask students to draw one of these when you think about the habitat around you. For example, more than one kind of herbivore will be eating any green plants in the habitat, and these in turn may be preyed upon by more than one predator.

Breaking the food web

Organize your students into a circle, giving all of them the name of some plants and animals in a local food web. One student alone stands in the centre and they represent the Sun. Tie the end of a ball of wool to their wrist, and then pass the ball to any members of the circle who represent green plants. This is the energy flow from the Sun to the producer. Now the green plants pass the ball in turn to any herbivores in the circle and they in turn pass the ball to any predators. With care the wool will stay taut and a kind of star is formed inside the circle. Now remove a student from the circle. Imagine an animal has been lost to the habitat. They dropped their wool and as a result the pattern is broken. The more organisms that break the food chain the more at risk other animals will be.

Presentation

Other students might enjoy a demonstration of the food web game. Students can present to each other their own examples of food webs and chains.

At home

WS 7

Ask students to look for examples of food webs in and around their own homes.

Ask students to complete WS 7, possibly as homework to revise food chains.

Plenary

Ask students to think about their place in different food chains. Could they ever become prey, rather than predator?

Unit 1: Interdependence and adaptation – Plant producer

The objectives for this lesson are that students should be able to:

- Understand that almost all food chains begin with a green plant

- Learn that green plants capture and use energy from the Sun

- Learn that green plants are called producers

- Understand that, without producers, there could be no food chains and no life.

SB pp.10–11

Starter

- Bring some processed food into school – cheese, for example. Open a similar conversation to that below, to get the students to engage with the relationship between plants and the food chain. *It's all made in a factory! It isn't? Well where did it come from? Cheese is made from milk? Well, that's made in a factory, isn't it? No? It comes from cows! Well cows live in factories, don't they? No? They live in fields! But there's nothing to eat there! There is? Grass? But I can't eat grass? Cows can? So how does the grass grow? Maybe that's made in a factory? No? It's a green plant and uses the energy of the Sun! So my cheese is the end of a chain that starts with the Sun.*

- Say that this process is called a food chain. Recall the chain – Sun, green grass, cows' milk, cheese.

Explain

Plants in the food chain

Almost all the energy that drives living things comes from the sun. Animals cannot make use of that energy directly, so they eat plants, which can. Food chains like this transfer energy. Green plants can make their own food; some animals (herbivores) eat green plants; some animals (carnivores) eat other animals. This is called a food chain. If a link is missing from the food chain, the rest of the chain is changed. Animals may be put in danger.

Most food chains are very short. Phytoplankton (planktonic plants) float in the lighter surface waters of the sea. They harness the sun's energy through photosynthesis to live and grow.

They produce oxygen as a waste product. The phytoplankton are food for other living things. Krill are small shrimp-like crustaceans that feed on phytoplankton. Whales feed by eating huge quantities of krill. (Blue whales can eat four tonnes of krill every day). This is a food chain.

Most of the energy in a food chain is lost at one level or another in respiration. So it cannot be passed on to the next link. By the time the whales have swallowed the krill, they will have lost a lot of the energy they gained, just by staying alive.

Food web

Food chains are seldom simple. Other creatures eat phytoplankton, including a lot of the sea's filter feeders – shellfish and small fishes. They might be eaten in turn by gulls, turtles and other sea creatures. These interlinking food chains become a food web.

Food chains show how plants are eaten by plant-eaters, and plant-eaters are eaten by meat-eaters. But it isn't quite as simple as that.

A food web shows the animals that might live on or around a tree, for example. In every food web, there are many different food chains. The food web in a woodland, for example, might involve some plant-eating consumers such as grasshoppers and mice. A secondary consumer like a frog might not tackle the mouse, but will make a meal of the grasshopper. Snakes are partial to frogs, but not averse to a mouse, or a grasshopper either.

So although the flow of energy through natural chains may be short, it is far from simple.

Make your own food

It's a thought-provoking lesson that, apart from vitamin D, which our skin can make from sunlight, we are unable to make a single bit of the food we need to live. We are animals, and animals need plants to provide them with food (and oxygen, as we have seen elsewhere).

Both plants and animals might move, but movement is one of the features that commonly identifies an animal. Movement is forced upon animals because they are incapable of making their own food. As a result, they might browse, moving from plant to plant, or actively hunt, seeking out their prey. A few do not move to find food; they anchor themselves and wait for food to come to them.

Invisible gas and tasteless liquid

It's one of the extraordinary facts of science that virtually every bit of the trees in a forest was manufactured by the trees themselves. The raw materials are a colourless, odourless, tasteless gas (carbon dioxide) and a colourless, odourless, tasteless liquid (water). Combining these simple sugars. Building on sugars, and sometimes adding other chemicals, produces both the material of trees and the energy to keep them alive.

Things to do

Collecting sunlight

Flowering plants range from the grasses to the tallest trees, stopping at all the garden favourites in-between. Green plants make their own food by photosynthesis from the raw materials of water and carbon dioxide. And for that, they need to catch the light of the sun. Their whole structure is aimed at collecting and using as much sunlight as possible.

This leads to a branching root system that can grip the soil (the roots of a tree are roughly the same size and extent as its canopy); a strong stem (sometimes a trunk) that can hold the leaves up high – and above the leaves of competitors – and a mathematically precise leaf pattern.

If you want to see the effectiveness of this leaf pattern, stand under a tree on a sunny day. The leaves are laid out to ensure that even the lower ones make use of the light missed by those above them. The result is a complete shadowing of the ground beneath a mature tree.

Teamwork

Both animals and green plants need oxygen to live. Both produce carbon dioxide gas. But in sunlight, green plants can take carbon dioxide and combine it with water, making the oxygen both will need.

Gases go into and come out from animals and green plants, in the day and at night. Both plants and animals respire all the time. But plants photosynthesise during the daylight hours, producing the oxygen we need to breathe. It's a good thing the plants are around; without them we would quickly run out of oxygen.

It seems very likely that life on Earth only really took off as the first green plants released oxygen into a lifeless atmosphere.

Dig deeper

Photosynthesis stops at night. Respiration doesn't. But if you can maintain light levels – for example, by growing plants under a 'light bank' – they will photosynthesise 24 hours a day.

Did you know?

Plants will grow in the dark (most seeds germinate underground) but they are down to their food reserves if they have no sunlight to use. They grow long and straggly and lose their green colour. This, incidentally, is called etiolation.

Start a new life!

You can grow trees from seed. You will need to be patient – plant a number of acorns or chestnuts in pots, water regularly and care for the tiny seedling. When it is too big for the pot, transplant it to a bigger one and finally plant it out somewhere where it can flourish.

Trees can live for a hundred years or more, sometimes much more. One thing is certain – you have a friend for life!

Adopt a tree!

As well as growing plants in the classroom, you can learn from studying plants in the local environment.

Get familiar with a mature, grown-up tree. You can learn more about a mature tree in lots of ways. If you can observe your tree from a window, stick a card frame on the window so that you can look through at it every day. If you are artistic, make a sketched record of it throughout the year. If you are a photographer, try a regular photo and see how the tree changes. Make a diary of a year in its life. If your tree is in danger from building or development, you will have evidence of the importance and beauty of your tree.

Presentation

There are great opportunities for presenting to other classes on the wonder of plant life. Research has shown that while all 8–11 year olds appear to agree that plants grow, only 69% of them regard plants as living. Prepare presentations to change that view.

Plenary

Reinforce the students' understanding of the importance of green plants to life on Earth, and our interdependence on plants – no matter where we live.

Unit 1: Interdependence and adaptation – Life in the soil

The objectives for this lesson are that students should be able to:

- Discover that different types of soil are found in different places

- Identify and group vegetables by using a key

- Understand that different organisms live in different types of soil

- Research how scientists group living organisms.

SB p.12–13

Starter

- Show a picture of a burrowing animal. *What other animals can you name that live in the soil? How are these animals adapted to living underground?*

- Collect some creatures from dark, damp conditions. This gives the students first-hand experience of the conditions these creatures can be found in.

- If you have some bedding plants, you could look at what happens if one of them isn't watered, showing how some plants need wetter conditions than others.

Explain

Is it all mud?

Small children often equate mud with mud pies; the mud being readily shaped. This means it needs to be wet and sticky. Some soils aren't like this. Some are dry and sandy. Some are rocky and dry. Letting the students experience different soils either just with their hands, or challenging them to a 'soil castle' making contest can be fun and also allows them to decide which soil is best for particular jobs.

Too wet or too dry

Different animals need different conditions to live in. The Mongoose lives in rocky, sandy soils so it can make its home. The earthworm needs vegetation-rich and slightly moist soil. It has mucus (slime) over its body that it uses to glide through the soil. It needs the soil to be moist to avoid the soil just sticking to it.

Scavenger plants

A scavenger is an animal that seeks out the leavings of other animals, or the remains of dead animals. It is not a true predator, as it doesn't hunt. Plants can be scavengers too. For instance, in the Arctic, some plant seeds can lie dormant for hundreds of years waiting for the right conditions to grow. When a dead animal decays the nutrients do not penetrate very far into the soil because it is frozen, but nearby dormant seeds will germinate and use the nutrients.

Things to do

Making a key

Many students will have already used keys and will also have been introduced to keys earlier in this section. This is an opportunity to practise both 'branching' and 'go to' key making skills, using soils and the organism that live in them as a stimulus.

Care needs to be taken when handling soils. It may be better to collect different soils yourself, including compost, sandy soil (sand and compost mixed) rock (sandy with rocks in but a high proportion of compost) and some alluvial, which will be very fine grained but almost water logged. Students could wear gloves when handling soil, but should always wash their hands afterwards.

Support

Provide students with a template for whichever key they chose. By providing them with some questions for a key, they could decide which order they go in. Questions might include:

How big are the particles? Are the particles big or small?

How wet is the soil? Is the soil wet or dry?

What colour is the soil? Is the soil brown or yellow?

Does the soil hold its shape?
These examples show that some 'go to' questions can also be turned into branching key questions.

Extend

Research different soils and produce fact cards about either the plants or the animals that live in them.

Record

The key is the record. There are a number of computer programs intended for branching identification keys.

Dig deeper

Students can explore the classification of plants and animals, and also learn 'What is classification?'

I wonder...

There is more than one answer to this question. Plants and animals have adapted to living in their habitat in different ways. Some plants growing in poor soils supplement the mineral nutrients by trapping and digesting insects. These carnivorous plants include sundews, Venus fly trap and various pitcher plants. Other plants have adapted and no longer need lots of nutrients for survival. Many herbs that grow in hot, dry and rocky soil conditions don't survive in well-watered, compost-rich soil.

Farmers and gardeners can alter the content of the soil by adding fertilizers that enable plants which thrive in richer soils to be grown successfully. They can also drain or irrigate the soil to create the right conditions for plants and be selective about what they plant.

Other ideas

Plant material

Some students could repeat some of the investigations from previous grades and topics on drainage, or do an investigation on soil settling, to examine how much humus is in the soil. Shake some soil in a tall vessel with water. Leave it to settle and the students will observe that the soil will separate out into layers. If a known amount of soil was used, the investigation can be repeated with other samples of the same size and the results compared directly. The larger stones will sink first and settle at the deepest level, with the finer material above it. Any plant material will usually float on the surface. The layers can be measured and a bar chart of soil structure produced.

Growing conditions

Seeds could be set to germinate in their ideal conditions, after discussion and agreement of what these are, but placed in different soils. The germination rate could be monitored to decide the best soil for the seeds. This could be set up as an investigation activity.

Presentation

The students could present their findings from the soil observation as if they were agronomists (people who examine soil and then recommend the nutrients that are needed to grow the best crops). They could also list the animals that were found in the soil and use PowerPoint to show pictures of the animals.

If they film the soil settling, this can be run to show the soil composition. They can make recommendations as to what they think the soil needs if the farmer wanted to grow a particular crop. (Rice, for example, needs a very wet soil.)

Encourage the students to draw pictures of the soil settling activity that can be labelled and displayed.

At home

Ask the students to look at the soil from a local garden and compare it with the samples examined in class. They can then decide on their soil type and predict the sorts of animals and plants that might be found in their garden.

Plenary

Look at the labels of some compost bags and soils. What do they contain? What sorts of plants are they recommended for? Plant nurseries have multipurpose compost, ericaceous compost, bark chips and leaf mould that can all be used as examples.

Unit 1: Interdependence and adaptation – Adapting to a habitat

The objectives for this lesson are that students should be able to:

- Explore how animals and plants are adapted to their own environment

- Find out where different plants and animals are found

- Compare two different habitats and the organisms that live in them

- Explain how plants and animals are suited to their own habitats.

SB pp.14–15

Starter

- Show pictures of the Galapagos Islands and the wildlife found there, showing the adaptations of the animals that Charles Darwin found. Look at a map and discuss how the animals got from one island to the next and why they did so. Discuss the work done by Darwin on the Galapagos Islands, especially his observations of the different-shaped beaks of the finches (matched to their food) and the different-shaped shells of the tortoises that have ensured survival on the islands.

- Discuss with the students how certain animals and plants might be adapted. A burrowing animal doesn't have good eyesight as it spends a lot of time underground. Birds that feed on the seashore have long legs to wade in the water. Some birds, such as penguin, have adapted their whole body shape to swim, and some plants are adapted to living in dry conditions. For instance, the thick stem of a cactus stores water.

Explain

How plants survive

Adaptation may need explaining to the students. Both plants and animals adapt to their environment.

Plants and animals adapt to ensure the best chance of survival wherever they live. A rainforest is full of animals and plants that are adapted to live in hot, humid conditions.

Now you see me, now you don't

Animals adapt to living in their particular habitat so they can survive. An animal that is hunted, like a hare, will use camouflage to enable it to come out of its burrow to eat, without being spotted by a predator. If the scenery changes quite drastically during the year, e.g. heavy snows in winter, then the same colour coat throughout the year makes them obtrusive, so over many generations some animals have evolved to grow a white winter coat and a brown summer coat.

Most animals moult in summer to grow a new, thicker coat for winter. This, along with a layer of fat just below the skin acts as good insulation from the cold.

Things to do

Different places for different animals

If you are unable to actually take the students to a different habitat that contrasts greatly with the ones they have been studying, use pictures, Internet research or texts to find out about the organisms that would be found in the chosen habitat.

Support

Some students may need help in locating information about the organisms in a different habitat. You could use pictures to show the organism in its habitat.

Extend

All students should recognize that seaweed and fish will not survive in any other habitat than the sea. Some students could go on to compare and contrast three habitats: the beach, home and school.

Record

The students could either produce a table of comparisons, or produce a drawing of each habitat, labelling the organisms and how they are suited to their habitat. These could be displayed.

Dig deeper

There are other habitats that can be explored for comparison, such as a termite mound and a rainforest.

Did you know?

Chameleons and other animals, especially sea creatures like squid and cuttlefish, can change colour rapidly. Some bottom-dwelling flatfish change more slowly to match their surroundings.

I wonder...

If the Poles melt, then the sea levels will rise. The ice at the Poles supports its own flora and fauna, and these organisms will be put at risk of extinction. Animals may try to migrate to higher altitudes looking for icy habitats but may not be successful.

Other ideas

Information

The students could produce information cards on the organisms living in each of the habitats they have compared. They could do this by hand or using a computer program such as PowerPoint. The results could form the basis of a display.

The information cards could also be used in a game that includes a large picture of the background habitat, e.g. soil, grass and a few trees for a field; water and some seaweed and rocks for the beach. The cards could be placed on the picture and the students could then ask each other whether the organism is suited to its position, explaining why or where it should be moved to.

Feeding time

The students could discuss the feeding relationships of all the organisms they have encountered in a habitat and form this into a food chain. They could compare the food chains both within and between habitats, finding the producer in each one. A list of the similarities and differences can be established. More able students can then build these food chains into food webs.

Presentation

The students could use their information cards to produce a PowerPoint presentation for younger students, showing how an animal or plant is suited to where it lives.

At home

Give each student the name of a plant and get them to research its habitat.

Plenary

Show the students a picture of a city. Suggest to them that the city is a habitat they haven't studied. Discuss how a bird from a country habitat might adapt to life in the city.

Unit 1: Interdependence and adaptation – Being responsible

The objectives for this lesson are that students should be able to:

- Explore how animals and plants are adapted to their own environment

- Find out where different plants and animals are found

- Compare two different habitats and the organisms that live in them

- Explain how plants and animals are suited to their own habitats.

SB pp.16–17   *Starter*

- Show a range of images that illustrate how a local environment has changed over time. Discuss the differences: for example, increased building, loss of natural suroundings, loss of a habitat and the impact of this on the species that live there. Discuss whether this is good or bad and why. Students may consider that everything we do is 'bad', but they need to consider also the needs that we have for making life better for ourselves too.

- In contrast you could show images of how a park or landscape has been created to provide shelter and food for particular species, for example leaving 'wilder' areas in parks for insects and small mammals to forage in.

Explain

Where have all the flowers gone?

Cutting down trees (logging) in the rainforests can destroy over 250 species of plant with every acre of trees cut down. Orchids were prized in the 1800s by collectors, who would collect every example then burn the forest, to prevent other plant hunters from getting one. This not only destroyed the orchids' habitat, but also many other plant and animals species. Since the 1970s many orchids have had protected status.

Step back in time

When looking at technological advances made by humans, it can be easy to forget that new phones, computers, cars and televisions, not to mention improved sanitation, are very modern developments and not always necessary for everyday life.

While students may be aware of technology, the use of fossil fuels may be newer to some of them. Look at the globe and mark the richer nations; are they doing more to protect or destroy the environment?

Things to do

Where is the Dodo?

Human activity has led to more animal extinction than any other single factor.

The extinction of the Dodo is a classic case of human intervention. Scientists even tried to keep a few Dodos in captivity once they realized that the Dodo was endangered, but they didn't really understand what the Dodo ate, so fed it the wrong food. The captive Dodos died as they got fat and didn't breed.

In 1973 scientists found that there were only 13 tambalacoque trees left on Mauritius. It was discovered that the Dodo ate seeds from the tree. Digestion started to break down the outer casing of the seed so that it could germinate. But without the Dodos the seeds could not germinate. Research led to the turkey being used to eat the seeds as they have a similar digestive system. For the first time in over 300 years, the 'Dodo' tree, as it has become known, is having its seeds germinated after ingestion by turkeys.

The students could use this information and their research to create a timeline of the events that lead to the destruction of the Dodo, but also consider how human intervention caused its extinction.

Another animal hunted to extinction by man is the Quagga, a half-striped horse related to the zebra. The last one left alive in the world died in a zoo in Amsterdam in 1883. Scientists didn't realize it was a separate species of zebra as there was some confusion about the classification of zebra at that time. So this extinction came about through ignorance and a mistake.

Despite our best efforts, species are becoming extinct at an estimated rate of 150 a day. The creation of a seed bank should ensure that some endangered plant species survive.

Did you know?

There are many projects in the world to save rare or endangered species, not just the Kew Gardens

Seed Bank; for example coral reefs in Australia and gorillas in the Congo. The students should be encouraged to research other ways in which we are trying to save species and their environments.

Dig deeper

Humans have been hunting animals and plants for thousands of years. It is only since about the 1900s that we have taken an interest in the diversity of species within our environment.

Wangari Maathi was a Kenyan environmental activist, and Kenya's deputy minister of environment, natural resources and wildlife. She won the Nobel Peace Prize in 2004 and is known for her initiative to plant trees in areas of Kenya suffering from deforestation.

Other ideas

Fossil fuels and mining

Humans have an impact on the environment around them, from mining and producing spoil heaps and large holes in the ground, to burning the coal that some mining activities produce.

Students could produce a list of all the things that require fossil fuels and then consider what would happen if we didn't have them anymore, for example motor cars, electricity, etc.

Students could find out more about what things are mined and discuss mining for non-essential items, like diamonds.

What if...?

You could carry out a 'what if...?' question to help illustrate this as part of your Starter. Start with something like *'what if... I chop down that tree?'* then ask the students to consider all the consequences and then the consequences of these and then continue until you get an almost outlandish answer! This shows the impact that one thing can have on another, similar to the 'butterfly effect' where one small action leads to much larger ones.

Nature takes over

For 200 years, the peppered moth in England changed from a quite pale form to a much darker version, as it adapted to its habitat. The reason for the change was the Industrial Revolution and the pollution it caused. Many buildings and places where the peppered moth landed were covered in soot, so the darker moth was camouflaged. This meant the pale version went into decline. Now, with cleaner industry, both types of moth are living alongside each other. The students could discover what other organisms have adapted to man's changes rather than been destroyed.

Uno's Garden by Graeme Base is a childrens' story book which gives a great insight into the changes that humans make over time to an environment.

Presentation

Prezi is a useful online tool for presenting a slide show. It allows students to place all their ideas on a virtual piece of paper and then create a slide show from this, as an alternative to using PowerPoint or other tool within school.

Drama and plays can be used to show other classes what impact humans have had.

Students could start a research project on an endangered organism, e.g. Siberian Tiger; Chinese Alligator; Pygmy Hippo; Giant Panda, etc. Use the Internet to research other endangered species.

These species are endangered mainly because of human actions, but are being protected now. This could be presented in many ways, including drama, booklet, PowerPoint, etc.

At home

Survey family members as to what the place they were born in looked like when they were children and how it compares to today. Students could list the differences and discuss how humans have effected the changes.

Plenary

Share some images of buildings that have been abandoned, and wilder road verges. What do students notice about how they have changed from when they were first built. Discuss how nature will claim back things if given a chance.

You could also look at new species that have been discovered by scientists as they evolve to fill the new niches that humans create when they change the environment.

Unit 1: Interdependence and adaptation – What a load of rubbish!

The objectives for this lesson are that students should be able to:

- Understand the importance of the '3 R's'

- Find out how they can care more for the environment

- Understand, as a class and individual, how they can reduce the amount of waste they produce

- Explore why caring for the environment is important.

SB pp.18–19   *Starter*

- Ask the question: *If you saw a piece of litter on the floor – would you pick it up? Why?* Students discuss their ideas.

- Provide a rubbish bag for each group of students and tip out the contents onto the table. Make sure the contents are clean! You could include a range of items, for example cereal packets and boxes, polystyrene plates, tins and bottles, (glass and plastic) and newspapers. Challenge the students to sort the items into those that can be recycled, reused or reduced. You may need sorting hoops, or Venn diagrams to complete this if there is an overlap of items. The students can also check the packaging to see what it is made from, if it has already been recycled or if it can be.

> ⚠ Provide plastic gloves or antibacterial handwash for after this event. Discuss reducing the amount of rubbish we send to landfill and throw in the general waste.

The film *Wall-E* is based on the concept of humans not caring for their environment and a sequence may provide a good way to introduce this topic. It could lead to creative writing in terms of producing different endings to the story – if the humans *hadn't* learned from their mistakes what might have happened? Did students change their behaviour after seeing the film?

Explain

Reducing pollution

Pollution can take many forms, including litter, chemicals getting into waterways and killing fish and other organisms, and climate pollution with carbon dioxide contributing to global warming (although this is a contentious issue as the Earth has periodically, over millions of years, heated up and cooled down). There is even pollution in space! Rockets and shuttles jettison their waste into space, and it then continues to orbit the Earth. What would happen if this continued?

The rubbish dump

Use the rubbish bag from the Starter, to encourage the students to work out the percentages of rubbish in your bag that could be removed for reduction, recycling or reuse. Is this possible on a daily basis?

Investigate either with real bins around the school (health and safety risk assessments need to be followed) or carry out a 'litter pick' in a designated area and then calculate the waste percentages.

Things to do

Recycling in the classroom

Many schools are now becoming involved with recycling. The cycle seems to be that economies grow, produce more waste, then realize what impact it is having on the environment. They then take steps to reduce this impact. Often this starts in schools. If your school doesn't have recycling bins, this is an ideal opportunity to start recycling. If your school already has a green policy then this could be stepped up further. The students could research further into what happens to the recycled waste once it is collected and use this information in posters to help encourage others to recycle.

Reusing in the classroom

The 'reuse' orchestra is fun. You could make it more challenging by asking the students to produce a recognizable tune from their instruments.

Reducing in the classroom

Paper that has been used on one side can be used on the other side as well, reducing the overall amount of paper consumed.

There are other ways to reduce too. Turning off taps and putting plastic bottles or bricks into water cisterns can reduce the amount of water used.

Did you know?

Turning off lights reduces the amount of electricity we use. This in turn reduces the amount of energy that power stations need to produce, and in so doing pollutes the atmosphere less. Using green power (produced by solar or wind farms) is better for the environment. Fresh water is a valuable commodity in hot countries. Sometimes it can only be provided by desalination.

I wonder...

If we don't recycle or try to reduce our waste, we could end up with bigger rubbish dumps. These could lead to disease from the animals that scavenge from the dumps. Eventually there would be no space left for any more rubbish dumps.

Dig deeper

Plastic bottles can be recycled and used to generate electricity. Energy from one recycled plastic bottle can light a bulb for about three hours.

Years ago, before plastic bags and cars, people bought what they could carry in their arms or in baskets that they used again and again.

Other ideas

Lights out

Students could produce posters to go by light switches and other electronic devices to encourage them to be turned off completely either at the end of the day or when not being used.

Alternative sources of electricity

There are other ways in which our electricity can be generated, e.g. wind, solar, ground heat source, water, etc. By researching each of these the students could then explain which would be best to replace coal and fossil fuelled power stations for electricity generation. This could be in the form of a presentation.

What if...

We didn't save energy or recycle? What would happen to our world?

Dig deeper

Plastic can be recycled as fibres and used for fabrics and clothing – fleeces, for example.

Presentation

The information researched about energy consumption in the school could be displayed as data and also presented in a school assembly with guidance on what is to be done to reduce this.

The students could produce a newspaper report about their school's energy consumption and what they are going to do about it.

At home

Carry out a survey of ways in which each family cares for the environment by reducing water, electricity and rubbish that they use. Present the results as a chart. Do this later in the year as well, to see if there are any changes in habits in families.

Plenary

Challenge the students to use their 'reuse' orchestra to write and perform a song about caring for the environment, including the phrase, 'reduce, reuse, recycle'.

Unit 1: Interdependence and adaptation – Unit 1: Review

The objectives for this lesson are that students should be able to:

- Check what they have learned about interdependence and adaptation in this unit

- Find out how they are working towards, within and beyond the Grade 6 level.

SB p.20   *Expectations*

Students working towards Grade 6 will:

- recognize that a green plant needs light and water to grow well

- that different animals and plants live in different habitats

- recognize that some animals feed on other animals and some on plants

- use keys to identify some animals and plants

- make predictions about what will happen.

In addition, students working within Grade 6 will:

- recognize that a green plant needs light and water and air to produce new material

- describe how animals in two habitats are suited to the conditions

- represent feeding relationships in food chains beginning with a green plant

- understand and use the terms producer, consumer, predator and prey when talking about feeding relationships

- start to create keys to identify animals and plants

- recognize the impact humans have on their environment – both good and bad

- use a wide range of resources to find things out

- decide on the most appropriate way to present information

- say how their evidence supports their prediction.

Further to this, students working beyond Grade 6 will also:

- recognize that green plants are the original source of food for almost all animals and that they produce material for new growth from air and water in the presence of light.

Check-up

Discuss with the students how the Go for Green Club can make the area better, e.g. clear out the rubbish and cut back the overhanging trees. They could add compost to the soil to make it less sandy or use fertilizer to help the plants grow better. They will also need to ensure that they water well so that the plants don't die of thirst in the very free-draining sandy soil.

They should also discuss what they could turn the rubbish into, e.g. tyres could become plant pots in the form of raised beds; bottles can carry water to the plants; plastic bags can be tied to sticks to scare birds away from delicate seedlings.

Assessment   **WS 9**   **WS 10**

Use the Unit 1 assessment on WS 9 and WS 10 to check the students' understanding of the content of the unit. The answers are given opposite.

Name: _____   Date: _____

WS 9 Unit 1 assessment 1

1

owl   tree   Sun   finch   grasshopper

a) Write this food chain in order. Draw arrows to show the energy flow.

b) Where does the producer get its energy from? _____

c) Name the primary and secondary consumer in this food chain.

The primary consumer is: _____

The secondary consumer is: _____

2 a) If you pour water on to soil, it will pass through. Some soils let water pass through faster than others.

A   B   C   D

Which soil drains best: A, B, C or D? _____

Unit 1: Interdependence and adaptation   9

Name: _____ Date: _____

WS 10 Unit 1 assessment 2

b) The graph shows how much water each type of soil let through in five minutes.

Volume of water (cm³)

soil A soil B soil C soil D
Soil type

Which of these soils was sandy? _____

Which was a clay soil? _____

c) Marram grass grows in very sandy places. Explain how the long roots of the marram grass help it to survive in very sandy places.

_____
_____
_____

3 Aden was puzzled. 'Where do trees get all the stuff to grow so big?' she said. 'Does it come from the soil?' Answer her.

_____
_____
_____

10   Heinemann Explore Science Grade 6

The answer!

Refer back to the original question on why the river will suffer if fertilizers and pesticides are washed into it. This is a form of pollution, although many students may think the fertilizer will help plants to grow well. In these conditions, some plant populations explode, so that they stifle other plants and prevent them from growing well. This affects the wildlife that may have been dependent on one or more of the stifled plants. Also, the pesticides might kill insects that form a valuable link in the food chain. The water will also flow less well, so less dissolved oxygen will reach the organisms that live in the river, and they will suffer from a lack of oxygen.

And finally...

Make a display of a habitat visited by the students with pictures of the organisms that live there. The students can write labels explaining how the organisms have adapted to their habitat and what they eat or are eaten by. Arrows can be placed to show the feeding relationships. As these will not be in neat lines, this will demonstrate how plants and animals are part of food webs, showing that some plants are eaten by a variety of animals and that animals eat a varied diet.

Answers

1   **a**   Sun → leaf → grasshopper → sparrow → owl.

    b   The Sun.

    c   The primary consumer is the grasshopper; the secondary consumer is the sparrow.

2   **a**   C.

    b   Sandy – soil C   Clay – soil D.

    c   The long roots of marram grass help to anchor it in the sand, and also help it to gather moisture over a wider area.

3   The material that trees are made from is created from the starch made by photosynthesis and small amounts of minerals absorbed from the soil through the roots.

Unit 2: Scientists

The objectives for this Unit are that students should be able to:

- Name some famous scientists and what they discovered

- Understand that science is always adapting as new discoveries are made

- Plan careful scientific investigations and make accurate measurements

- Say how the evidence they collect supports any prediction made

- Evaluate and learn from the work of other scientists.

SB p.21   Science background

It is unlikely that many of your students will become traditional, white-coat scientists. However they will all need and value the skills their science education gives them to understand the modern world, to make sound decisions and to avoid being misled by the pseudo-sciences. At present, science is the best way we have of understanding the way the world works.

Science demands evidence – proof that what is concluded is true. And one of its strengths is that existing science can be proved wrong; or at least to be only telling a partial truth. Ideas are questioned; laws are broken. The new ideas bring us a step nearer to the truth. So science is always changing. It is not set in stone – and that's what makes it so exciting. It means that you, or any of your students, could make the next big step forward. Science does not belong to the scientists.

So two of the scientists discussed in this Unit are children. One asked a question about the behaviour of water that still baffles scientists. Another made an observation – and a link – that changed every long-haul flight in the world. And you will find that Albert Einstein – when still a boy – asked a question that, when he was finally able to answer it, led to his famous theory of relativity.

Many people have the idea that scientists are lonely eccentrics struggling with irrelevant experiments; or homicidal maniacs bent on death and destruction. Neither picture is true. Most scientists work in teams, with people of both sexes, all nationalities and increasingly – especially with

the growth of the Internet – from all over the world. So one of the scientists in this Unit lived in Iraq while another, Brunel, was British, but the son of a Frenchman, and Albert Einstein was, of course, originally Austrian.

Scientists often live very ordinary lives, have families and friends, love sport, gardening and the arts, and may or may not have a religious faith or be politically active. In short, scientists are normal. But they have never lost that child-like wonder that leads them to ask questions, to explore and sometimes to discover. Isaac Newton, perhaps the greatest scientist of all, recognized his own insignificance – and the world that's still out there to discover:

'I was like a boy playing on the sea-shore, and diverting myself now and then finding a smoother pebble or a prettier shell than ordinary, whilst the great ocean of truth lay all undiscovered before me.'

Language

Carbon dioxide	Colourless, odourless gas produced by the respiration of living things; combined with water by plants in photosynthesis.
Engineer	A person who applies science to design, construction and maintenance.
Scientist	Someone who asks questions and carries out tests to find the answers.
Reflection	Light that has bounced from a surface.

Resources

- bucket

- pencil

- coins

- yoghurt pots or conical plastic cups

- wool or thin string

- glue

- ice tray

- freezer access

- art materials.

Bright ideas

- Invite students to 'draw-a-scientist'. Ask them to imagine what a scientist looks like, what they wear and what they do. Ask them to draw the kind of things scientists use. Discuss the pictures. Let the students talk about them. Don't expect anything but stereotypes! You are likely to get 'Professor Branestawm' characters, with Einstein hair and flasks of bubbling chemicals. This is because the activity is very like asking students to draw a dragon. There are certain characteristics that are used to define a scientist – male, white, coat, glasses, bald head – and students may use these to define their version. (Though you may get the trendy young scientist too – male or female – who decorates some modern TV programmes.) Keep the pictures, so that at the end of the Unit you can ask how their attitude to scientists has changed.

- Ask students to collect current newspaper and/or Internet stories involving science and scientists. Group them – some may be scare stories, others will concern the environment, others new medical advances. In most cases, it is the use or abuse of science, rather than science itself, that is to blame for science getting a poor press.

Skills check

Students need to:

- make careful observations and measurements

- collect evidence and decide how good it is

- realize when it is useful to use secondary sources

- say whether their evidence supports any prediction made

- use results to draw conclusions and to make further predictions

- generalize from their results.

Some students will:

- consider how scientists have combined evidence from observation and measurements with creative thinking to suggest new ideas and phenomena.

Knowledge check

- Students should have some general knowledge of the work of scientists.

- Students should have some personal experience of the work of scientists – most likely in the health professions.

Let's find out...

The Unit opens with a question from Zach Bjornson-Hooper, a thirteen year old from Alamo, USA. His discovery may not compare with the Principle of Relativity, but it could be a good deal more important to you! Zach had noticed that he and his family had stomach trouble after long flights. They put it down to foreign food and jet-lag, but Zach noticed that water on the flight was served from jugs, and concluded that it must have come from a tank somewhere.

Unit 2: Scientists – Alhazen and how we see

The objectives for this lesson are that students should be able to:

- Understand that scientists come from different times and cultures, and are both women and men

- Discover how combining observation with imagination has helped to explain what we experience every day

- Find out how scientists such as Alhazen tested his theories

- Carry out investigations of their own and evaluate the results.

SB pp.22–23

Starter

- Discuss how we see. How do our eyes work? Why do we need light? Why can't we see in the dark? (Caution – few students have experienced true darkness, and because they think of their low-light bedroom as dark, assume they can see in darkness.)

Ask students what they would see if they took a black and white cat into a dark cupboard. (You could try it if you had an amenable cat!) Many will expect to see 'its white paws'; most will expect to see its eyes, since they appear to shine like lights. Ask what the cat will see, too!

Explain

How do we see?

Because students seldom experience total darkness, they may have trouble with understanding basic concepts about seeing. It is important to remember that the eye is a receptor of light, not a source of it. Despite our everyday phrases like 'piercing eyes' and 'peering through', our eyes are passive receptors. It was an Arab scientist, Alhazen, around 1000 years ago, who determined that we saw because of reflected light. Before him, there was a general belief that light from a source and some mysterious beams from our eyes fell on an object at the same moment, enabling us to see it.

We need a light source to see in the dark; and we see because light is reflected from everything to a greater or lesser extent – better from mirrors and shiny surfaces, and from white surfaces, too; poorly from black and dark surfaces. Modern 'super-reflectives' – such as road signs and the armbands students wear – reflect a very high proportion of light falling on them, and so appear to shine with their own light. But they don't. Like the eyes of a cat, they reflect back the light shining on them. Nocturnal creatures such as cats need to make the best use of low light. Their eyes are lined with a reflective surface so that light falling on their eyes goes through the retina twice. It is this reflection that makes their eyes 'glow in the dark'. But they are not light sources. Cartoon characters with magic beans from their eyes, or whose eyes light up in a dark cupboard, do not help correct this misconception.

Light is all around us. Sunlight is reflected from clouds, and the surfaces all around us. So sunlight fills our daytime lives from every direction. The back of the house may be shady, but the rooms are not totally dark because the Sun's light is reflected into them. We live our lives in a sea of sunlight.

Things to do

Bend some light

When lights passes through materials such as glass, water or plastic, it slows down. As light enters and leaves a glass lens, it changes speed and direction. This is called refraction and is the basis of lenses. The Roman emperor, Nero, made use of refraction to view performances in the arena through a fragment of emerald just the right shape to aid his failing eyesight. Activities that put a pencil, or a stick, in water, show how their image is bent when the light passes through the water.

Did you know?

Students love facts about eyesight. They can research optical instruments. Robert Grosseteste, whose ideas inspired Roger Bacon, noticed that refraction through fragments of glass enlarged grains of sand in the 1160s, and this led to the lens. Around the year 1200, an Italian monk put two lenses in a frame to make the first spectacles. In 1887, Louis Girard of Houston, Texas, developed the first contact lens. His model covered the whole eye; but a broken one covering the cornea only worked just as well.

I wonder...

There are honey guides on the surface of petals – lines that guide insects to nectar. They are only visible in ultraviolet light. Snakes can use infrared light to stalk warm-blooded animals in low light.

Other ideas

Why is the sky blue? Why are sunsets red? Using a little milk in a jar of water, you can demonstrate how light is scattered, giving the sky its colour. You need a clear, straight-sided drinking glass or clear plastic or glass jar, water, milk, measuring spoons and a torch. This activity needs to be carried out in a darkened room.

Fill the glass or jar about two-thirds full of water. Add half to one teaspoon (2–5 ml) milk and stir. Take the glass and torch into a darkened room.

First, hold the torch about the surface of the water and observe the water in the glass from the side. What do the students see? Then hold the torch to the side of the glass and look through the water directly at the light. What do the students see? Finally, put the torch under the glass and look down into the water from the top. What do the students see? The small particles of milk suspended in the water scatter the light from the torch, like the dust particles and molecules in the air scatter sunlight. When the light shines in the top of the glass, the water looks blue because you see blue light scattered to the side. When you look through the water directly at the light, it appears red because some of the blue was removed by scattering. In outer space, the sky is black because there is no atmosphere. But particles in our atmosphere – air and dust – scatter the light. Blue light has the shortest wavelength. It is scattered more easily than the other colours and we see the sky coloured blue! Did the evidence match their predictions?

Water clocks

Water clocks are easily made with small holes in disposable containers like yoghurt pots. Ask students how they can measure an exact time in seconds.

(They can vary the amount of water in the upper container, or, much harder, vary the size of the hole.)

With a little imagination, they can make a water clock timer. Put a float in the water and arrange it so that it sends out a message – a floating flag, for example.

Presentation

It may be appropriate to ask the students to research some scientific words that have their origins in Arabic science.

Almanac	from an Arab word describing the phases of the Moon
Amber	Anbar
Cable	Habl
Cipher	Sifr
Cornea	Cornea
Diaphragm	Dayafergma
Earth	Eardh, Earz
Elixir	al-Aksir
Monsoon	Mawsim
Pancreas	Bankras
Safari	Safara
Sugar	Sukkar
Syrup	Shurb, Sharab

At home

Ask students to research other Arab scientists. Abbas ibn Firnas was a musician who took an interest in flight – making a pair of wings from feathers on a wooden frame in the ninth century. Other Arab scientists laid the foundations for our understanding of the circulation of the blood.

Plenary

Go back to the draw-a-scientist pictures. Do the students want to make any changes?

Unit 2: Scientists – Brunel and the railways

The objectives for this lesson are that students should be able to:

- Understand that some scientists are engineers

- Discover how engineers such as Brunel imagine things which did not exist before

- Carry out an experiment to test how train wheels stay on the track

- Predict what they might find and say if the evidence supports the prediction.

SB pp.24–25 — **Starter**

- Show the portrait of Isambard Kingdom Brunel in the *Student Book* – enlarged if at all possible. Copies are available on the Internet. This famous portrait of Brunel, taken in 1857, shows him at fifty years of age and at the height of his powers. The photographer, Robert Howlett, used the Fox Talbot photographic method to take pictures like this. The poisonous chemicals he used almost certainly led to Howlett's early death the following year.

Explain

What can you learn from a picture?

Look at Isambard Kingdom Brunel.

This is not a modern photograph. The sepia tint and absence of colour, as well as the clothes, tell you that this was taken some time ago. Photography was a Victorian development. When this man was alive, Queen Victoria was on the throne of England.

The clothes – the waistcoat, wing collar, bow tie and tall 'stovepipe' hat – are those of a wealthy Victorian. He has a pocket watch with a chain and fob – not a wristwatch. This is a rich man. His trousers and boots are dirty. This is a man who works with things, and his clothes are stained with the mud of a shipyard. His hands are in his pockets, and he looks full of life and energy. This is a practical, working man – an engineer.

Brunel is smoking a cigar – not a common twenty-first-century activity. In fact that strap carries a bag of spare cigars he takes everywhere. Behind him are the giant chains that will slow the huge ship he has designed, the *Great Eastern*, when it is launched. He doesn't know now, as he is photographed, that the launch will be a disaster and that in front of thousands of paying spectators, these chains will whip out of control, throwing a shipyard worker to his death. (See 'I wonder...') On the eve of its first sailing, Brunel himself will suffer a stroke. He will never look so strong and confident again.

In 1833, at the age of 27, Brunel was appointed as surveyor and engineer to the Great Western Railway between Bristol and London in the UK. Work began in 1835. People doubted that a railway line could be built that long. Brunel was confident, and also suggested a steamship from Bristol in the UK to New York in the USA, calling that the *Great Western* too. He had a tunnel, two miles long, dug near Bath. 4000 men and 300 horses were needed. In 1851, the line opened at a total cost of £6,500,000. The line was extended through Cornwall to Penzance, with bridges, viaducts and tunnels, including the Prince Albert Bridge over the River Tamar at Saltash. But when the prince formally opened it in 1859, Brunel himself was dying. The work and worry of the *Great Eastern* – by whose huge chains he had been photographed two years before – were killing him. He was told of a fatal explosion on the ship. Six days later, he died.

Things to do — WS 11

Faster and faster

The completed table in the *Student Book* looks like this. Some rounding is necessary.

Date	Vehicle	Time	Km per hour
1784	Stagecoach	16 hours	12
1837	Improved stagecoach	11 hours	17
1851	First steam train	4.5 hours	42
1912	Fast train	2 hours	95
2003	Modern express	1.5 hours	127

How train wheels stay on the track

The conical set of wheels works by self-correcting. As the wheel set wanders to one side, it puts the larger circumference of the wheel on that side onto the track. The wheel on that side is now travelling further for every revolution than the wheel on the other side. It might get ahead of its twin; but it pushes back towards the middle. The wheel set travels straight. This is a fixed set of wheels; the wheels are not free to move separately. The same thing happens on the bends. The outside wheel begins to run on the large circumference. This pushes the wheel back towards the track centre. The wheel set can take a gentle curve. If the wheel set negotiates a tight curve, then the flange on a railway wheel comes into play, keeping the train on the track. The flange isn't needed for most curves.

Use WS 11 to help the students investigate this, using cardboard tubes or plastic cups glued together. They should make their rail track from a loop of taut string held apart by equal blocks at each end. Ensure that they make their predictions before trying it out.

The result is counter-intuitive. If you ask students to predict the outcome, they will almost certainly choose the dumb-bell shaped wheels as this appears to 'hug' the track. Their prediction will not match the evidence – a valuable lesson.

Record

Photography was developing alongside Brunel's inventions, and the practical activities here present a great opportunity for recording using digital photography.

Support

Some students may need help – possibly a timeline – with placing Brunel in a historical context.

Dig deeper

Students could research the effect of friction on moving objects by looking on the Internet.

Did you know?

People were not used to travelling at the speed Brunel's railway could take them.

I wonder...

The *Great Eastern* was ill-fated. The launch was delayed and was unsuccessful; and the huge chains in the famous picture of Brunel whipped out to kill a workman.

Presentation

There are other portraits of Brunel on the Internet. Ask students to look carefully at the pictures of Brunel and think of words they would use to describe his character. They can present their ideas to the rest of the class.

At home

Ask students to imagine meeting Brunel. What questions would they like to ask him?

Plenary

WS 12 introduces another famous practical scientist, Florence Nightingale. She is regarded as the founder of the modern nursing profession. The circular results table is a reproduction of the way she actually recorded her mortality data. It is quite a difficult way of presenting her data. Discuss with the students why she might have chosen to present it in this way and how it could be improved.

WS 12

Unit 2: Scientists – You are a scientist

The objectives for this lesson are that students should be able to:

- Work in an organized and scientific way

- Learn how scientists work and begin to work that way themselves

- Explore how scientists use their imagination to question and explain the evidence they collect

- Research famous scientists and prepare a presentation on their adopted scientist.

SB pp.26–27   Starter

- Discuss the students' recent work in science. Were they really scientists? Maybe they didn't wear white coats – but they showed some good examples of the use of science skills. Isn't that science? Aren't they scientists?

Explain

Einstein and the speed of light

Scientists are human. They even write letters! All the letters ever written to or by Albert Einstein are stored in an archive in the Hebrew University of Jerusalem. Letters from fellow physicists and from admiring members of the public are filed alongside personal, racist and anti-Semitic abuse. One section is devoted to the letters of children. Whatever his feelings about the letters from adults, Einstein always made a point of replying to children. This principle led him to into a touching correspondence with Tyfanwy Williams, in 1946 a pupil at St Cyprian's Boarding School in Cape Town, South Africa.

'I cannot tell you how thrilled I was to receive your letter yesterday,' Tyfanwy wrote on the 19th of September. She wrote during a mathematics lesson. 'Outside the birds are singing and all that sort of thing, and here we sit and learn that x and y is equal to something divided by something else!' But her letter had brought her fame – 'The news that I had your signature went round the school in no time.'

Tyfanwy assured him that she was not disappointed to find that he was still alive. 'It's much nicer for one's favourite scientist in history

to be alive, than to know he died something like a century ago.' She told him about the Southern Cross, which she could see from her window: 'It's an awfully fine constellation and when I am feeling fed up at night after a day at school, I look at it and it cheers me up no end.'

She added: 'I forgot to tell you, in my last letter, that I was a girl. I mean I am a girl.' Although Tyfanwy had always regretted this, she was 'By now more or less resigned to the fact'. Einstein's reply was simple. 'I do not mind that you are a girl. But the main thing is that you yourself do not mind. There is no reason for it.'

Things to do

How fast does it freeze?

The answer to Mpemba's question is complex. When cold water freezes, it first forms a layer of ice on its surface, which acts as an insulator and slows down the freezing below it. Convection currents keep warm after moving, preventing this insulation layer from forming. Warm water also evaporates faster than cold. So more water is lost from the surface of a container of warm water than from a container of cold water; there is less water to freeze. And the process of evaporation is cooling too – your skin is cooled on hot days as your sweat evaporates. Mpemba had used wooden buckets for his ice cream. Wood is a good insulator – so much of this cooling had been by evaporation, not by loss through the bucket. Finally, heating water drives gases such as oxygen and carbon dioxide out of water. Impurities such as these lower the freezing point of water – as salt does on an icy road – and so would make cold water harder to freeze.

You can make ice cream very simply in the classroom, if you have access to plastic bags and lots of ice and salt. The students can then see the freezing process directly and also compare this process to the freezer or even Mpemba's wooden bucket.

Place some cream and sugar (approximately 4 teaspoons of sugar to a cup of cream) in a zip lock plastic bag. Place this bag inside a larger plastic bag with crushed ice and lots of salt in it. The bags need to shaken for about 10 minutes until the cream turns to ice cream. The process can be stopped at various times to examine the contents. And eat it afterwards! (Fruit juice flavourings are optional.)

The speed of light

There are artistic examples of how things might look at the speed of light on the Internet. Many illustrate the 'warp speed' effect of the Starship Enterprise. But Einstein's ideas are different, and can be applied to the way a familiar scene might look at close to the speed of light. There is an illustration (number 120) in Jacob Bronowski's book *The Ascent of Man*.

Did you know?

Einstein did not talk until he was three years old; but at twelve he taught himself Euclidean geometry. He did not enjoy school, using a family move as an excuse to avoid it for a whole year at age fifteen. He finally graduated in 1900 by studying the lesson notes of a classmate. He worked as a supply teacher for two years, and then in the patent office in Bern, of which he later said 'To tell the truth, most of the (inventions) now look pretty idiotic.' When American physicist Robert Andrews Millikan confirmed Einstein's theory on the behaviour of light almost a decade after Einstein first proposed it, he was surprised and unsettled by the unexpected result. Einstein's special theory of relativity was based on the realization that all our measurements of time and space depend upon human judgements on whether two distant events occur simultaneously. 'We conclude that a clock fixed at the Earth's equator will run slower by a very small amount than an identical clock fixed at one of the Earth's poles.'

I wonder...

It would not be surprising if a child asked a new question! But it would be unusual if it were one that could not be answered in the classroom. One question asked of a scientist by a child – as yet unanswered – is why only humans have developed language. But this is an opportunity to contact a real, living scientist – by letter, telephone or email – or have one visit the school, to offer an answer.

Other ideas

WS 12

Famous scientists

Among the people who have made contributions to our understanding of the world are men and women from many countries: Florence Nightingale, for example, was an Englishwoman born in Italy. Her work changed nursing and hospitals forever. Nightingale nurses became trained professionals, dedicated to the health of their patients. Nightingale hospital wards were places where people could get better. They had not been like that before. But Florence Nightingale was determined that 'a hospital should do the sick no harm'. Another major contribution was her invention of a form of 'pie chart' on WS 12. Florence's new chart showed how many soldiers were dying each month at Scutari Hospital in the Crimean War. The red sectors represented death from wounds. The bigger, blue sectors showed deaths from illnesses. At a glance, politicians could see that money spent on nursing saved more lives. Florence was the first to use charts like these to persuade people of the need for change.

Adopt a scientist

Zach's (referred to on page 21 of the *Student Book*) and Mpemba's work has been celebrated. It was very different a century and a half ago for the young Manya Slodovska – later to be named Marie Curie. She was fascinated by science from an early age. The occupying Russians forbad all 'higher studies' in Poland, which led her to study in another country – at the Sorbonne in France. Like Einstein, she asked challenging questions and sought out the answers. Students could adopt a scientist and find out, in particular, about their childhood and schooling.

Presentation

Ask students to prepare a presentation on their adopted scientist.

At home

Ask students to interview friends and relations – with their family's permission – who use science in their work in any way.

Plenary

Take some time to think about how thinking and attitudes have changed. Return to the 'draw-a-scientist' sheets. How would the students draw them now? What changes would they make? If there is time, re-draw them.

Unit 2: Scientists – Unit 2: Review

The objectives for this lesson are that students should be able to:

- Check what they have learned about scientists in this unit

- Find out how they are working towards, within and beyond the Grade 6 level.

SB p.28

Expectations

Students working towards Grade 6 will:

- recognize that scientists discover things.

In addition, students working within Grade 6 will:

- consider how scientists and engineers of the past have changed our lives with their creative thought

- use a range of resources to research

- present ideas clearly and communicate these with others

- recognize the skills that a scientist uses

- say if and how their evidence supports any prediction made.

Further to this, students working beyond Grade 6 will also:

- use their imagination and creative thought to develop their own ideas

- use prior knowledge and understanding to explain their own and others' ideas.

Check-up

Some classic science investigations are easy to repeat. You can use a prism to produce a

spectrum, as Isaac Newton did; or observe how things decay, like Louis Pasteur. But Mary Anning made her famous dinosaur discoveries while she was still a child; and more recently, Jane Goodall first observed a chimpanzee using a tool. Neither woman had any scientific training; both just observed, patiently. Students can do the same.

Assessment

WS 13

Use the Unit 2 assessment on WS 13 to check the students' understanding of the content of the unit. The answers are given opposite.

Name: _____ Date: _____

WS 13

Unit 2 assessment

1 a) Which of these people use science in their job: doctor, chemist, hairdresser, farmer, oil worker or pharmacist?

_____

b) Which of these scientists understand how medicines work and how much to give you? They give you the right amount with instructions on how to take them.

_____

2 Which scientist:

a) built a suspension bridge near Bristol in England? _____

b) first explained how we see things? _____

3 a) What force did Einstein predict could bend light? _____

b) What might be the source of this force? _____

c) What was happening in the sky when Einstein's prediction was proved? _____

4 Explain how any scientist you know about has used evidence and creative thinking to answer a scientific question.

_____
_____
_____

Unit 2: Scientists   13

Answers

1 **a** all of them use science; even the hairdresser, who must understand shampoos and bleaches.

   b doctor and pharmacist

2 **a** (Isambard Kingdom) Brunel

   b Alhazen

3 **a** gravity

   b a planet, moon or star

   c an eclipse of the Sun.

4 An explanation of how any scientist has used evidence and creative thinking to answer a scientific question.

The answer!

The Unit begins with the problem of Zach and the drinking water on aeroplanes. His family always drank bottled water when sailing their yacht, never from the tank, and they were never unwell. So Zach collected water samples from their next nine flights, and tested them at home. He described what he grew on sterile agar plates as 'smelling like rotten peanut butter'. Seven samples contained E. coli, faecal coliform and other bacteria. One contained insect eggs. His mother set about advising other passengers about drinking airline water. Now all water on long-haul flights is bottled.

And finally...

If it is possible to arrange a visit from a working scientist, this would be ideal. Prepare the person to talk about their job in a brief and interesting way. Pictures and safe examples of their work adds interest. Prepare the students to ask informed and revealing questions.

Unit 3: Humans

The objectives for this Unit are that students should be able to:

- Develop their understanding of the human body and its systems

- Collect appropriate evidence to test their ideas

- Understand how bodily systems work on their own and together

- Realize when it is useful to use secondary sources.

SB p.29 Science background

Research evidence suggests that students' understanding of their bodies and body organs is less accurate than you might suppose. Up to age nine, they may presume that the body is a hollow skin bag that is all 'stomach', containing food and blood and waste. Around age 11, they develop an understanding of digestion – 'lumps of food are broken down, and "goodness" is extracted' in the words of one researcher – so you can't assume significant prior knowledge; and you might start the Unit with concept mapping or some other evaluation.

The key systems to understand are the digestive and respiratory systems, together with the skeleton and muscles, heart and blood vessels visited previously in the *Keeping healthy* Unit in Grade 5.

All living processes need energy to work; and animals – including humans – obtain this energy, and the materials to build, maintain and renew their bodies from their food. The digestive system breaks down this food – physically by churning and squeezing, and chemically with acid and enzymes – so that it can be absorbed and used. The circulatory system carries this food and oxygen, and waste products including carbon dioxide, around the body. The respiratory system provides the oxygen needed to release the energy in every cell, and to expel the waste carbon dioxide produced. The muscles use this energy for activity, pulling on the bones and other organs of the body.

Other systems – the nervous system, the urinary and reproductive systems, have a vital role to play. Less well known are the endocrine – the hormone-producing 'balancing' system, and the defensive lymphatic system.

Language

Alveolus	Alveoli are like bunches of grapes where the gas exchange in breathing takes place.
Anus	The hole and muscular ring through which solid waste is expelled.
Appendix	A small 'dead end' in the gut, important to mammals like cows that digest the cellulose in plant cells.
Breathing	The physical process of taking air into the lungs and pushing it out again – a kind of gas exchange.
Diaphragm	A muscular sheet that separates the chest and abdomen.
Digestion	The breaking down of food to make nutrients available to the body.
Digestive enzymes	Chemicals that speed the breakdown of food without being changed themselves.
Large intestine	The colon; where water and salts are absorbed by the body, and faeces (feces) are formed.
Liver	The heaviest organ in the body at 1.5 kg, it helps store energy supplies, and breaks down fats. It also removes waste and toxins like alcohol from the blood, and manufactures some vitamins.
Lungs	The two spongy organs where oxygen is absorbed and waste carbon dioxide lost.
Oesophagus (American English: Esophagus)	The gullet – a 23 cm tube that links the mouth to the stomach.
Pancreas	18 cm long, it secretes digestive enzymes into the small intestine.
Respiration	The exchange of gases in your lungs and the release of energy in your cells.

Salivary glands	They secrete the liquid that lubricates and, in mammals, starts to break down the starches in foods to sugar.
Small intestine	The duodenum and ileum make up the small intestine. The duodenum is the short first part of the small intestine, and breaks down food for digestion. The ileum absorbs digested food through the 'fingers' that cover its walls.
Stomach	A churning muscular bag where acid and enzymes digest food.
Trachea	The windpipe, 10 cm long and 1.5 cm wide. This strong, flexible tube branches into the two lungs.

Resources

- *Humans* Reader
- roll of wallpaper
- pencils
- felt pens
- scrap paper
- a large plastic funnel
- a seashell, or a plastic cup
- stethoscope or wide plastic tube
- playground chalk
- hosepipe or rope, at least 8 m long
- hoops
- card
- tissue paper
- seconds timers or watches.

Bright ideas

- There are a number of resources that will enable students to place and name the main body organs. Plastic torsos are expensive, but lifelike. They are available in both sexes, and sexless, in a range of sizes and skin colours. Research cultural views on these 'naked' teaching aids before using them. They are sturdy, but collect dust quickly and can lose parts. There are repair and part replacement services available.

- Less expensive are the tunics to which fabric organs can be attached with Velcro. These are less lifelike, but teach size, shape and position well. Some have 'extendable guts' that will demonstrate the amazing length of the digestive system. There are optional 'diseased organs' kits, but these should not be used without careful consideration; some students may know sick people and heavy smokers.

Knowledge check

- Students should be able to name some body organs and have some idea of their function.

- Students should know that their torso is divided into two parts – an upper chest containing the heart and lungs, and a lower abdomen containing other vital organs.

- Students should know that we need food to grow, move, renew and repair our bodies, and what constitutes a balanced diet.

- Students should know that we need to breathe to live, and that our breath is drawn into our lungs and somehow changed there.

- Students should know that we need energy to live and especially to be active, and that we get that energy from our food.

Skills check

Students need to:

- make careful observations and measurements
- collect evidence and decide how good it is
- realize when to use secondary sources
- say whether their evidence supports any prediction made
- use results to draw conclusions and to make further predictions
- generalize from their results.

Some students will:

- consider how scientists combine evidence from observation and measurements with creative thinking to suggest new ideas and phenomena.

Let's find out...

The Unit opens with a question:

'What I don't understand,' said Ahmed, 'is why my heart beats faster–and my lungs work harder–JUST when I need all my energy to run!'

Unit 3: Humans – Where are your organs?

The objectives for this lesson are that students should be able to:

- Understand that their body is made up of many different organs, with different jobs to do

- Make and label a picture of the main body organs

- Correctly use the scientific names for these organs

- Design and make a presentation on the digestive system using ICT.

SB pp.30–31 — *Starter*

Play the **'Head and shoulders, knees and toes'** song and do the actions. Ask the students to point to parts of their bodies where they think some common organs are, such as the heart, lungs, stomach and brain and use these terms instead of the traditional words.

Ask some key questions like:

- *Where does our food go?*
- *What does our heart do?*
- *What would happen if we didn't have a heart?*

This should review students understanding of what our heart does.

Provide a blank outline of a human body on a piece of A4 paper, and ask students to draw what they think happens to food when we eat it. Discuss with them what organs they place in the body and where they place them.

Explain

A lot of bits/A lot of jobs/What's its name?

This section starts to introduce that there are cells in the body and that these cells are organized into organs. Many organs may well be known to the students and these they will try to draw in the following activity. Some organs are not instantly recognizable, like the skin. Students may not also recognize the mouth as an organ either.

Asking the students to imagine their body without the organs they already know about can lead to interesting discussions about what the function of the organ is. *Imagine not having a mouth, skin, a heart...etc.*

One discussion that could be started now and carried on later is whether blood is an organ. It is made up of different types of cells that work together, so could be classed as one. However the true definition of an organ is a collection of different tissues working together. A tissue is a collection of the same cells working, together e.g. muscle cells working together to make muscle tissue. The muscle then might work with other different tissues, e.g. in the heart there is muscle, as well as connective tissue.

Things to do

Where everything is

Ask students to work in pairs or groups. Give each group a pencil and a set of felt pens and a large sheet of paper – perhaps cut from an old roll of wallpaper. One student lies on their back on the paper and the other draws round them – with the pencil, which will not mark clothes. Then all the students set to work drawing and colouring in all the body systems they know. They use labels and colours to make their work clearer. They can display and present their 'body maps'. Then the maps are stored for the end of the unit, when they can be revisited to see what has been learned.

How big is it all?

Students can produce life-size pictures of some organs. These can be compared for size to the ones they drew on their body outline. This will help to illustrate why the organs have to sit on top of each other.

Record

Students naming and recording their body organs will need outlines to complete.

Support

Encourage students to make a handbook or user's guide to their body.

Extend

Students could look in the media for the frequent (sometimes contradictory) advice given on good health and present their discoveries and opinions.

Dig deeper

Students could find out more about different body systems including the nervous, endocrine and immune systems. They could revise work on skeletons and muscles from Grade 4.

Did you know?

These facts about the body extend students' understanding.

I wonder...

The appendix is a hangover. It presumably once had a function, but now, like ear lobes, it serves no very useful purpose. In fact, it can get infected rather easily, and can cause trouble. There may be students in the class who have experienced this.

Other ideas

Staying alive

What do you need to stay alive? Ask the students to imagine that they are on a desert island; what do they need to survive? Tell them the story of a survivor. What did they need? Have the students remembered the importance of air? Ask them to tell a modern castaway story, in writing, acting or pictures.

Noisy body

Everyone's body makes all sorts of noises. Some are quiet. Some are loud. Some can be embarrassing. In this activity, you can listen to some of those body noises, and decide what's making them! Ask students to listen at different places on a friend's body, putting the wide end of a funnel against their skin. Write down what they hear. Here are some words to help.

rumbling	sloshing	swishing
thumping	grumbling	beating

Now try:

1   Against their stomach just below their chest while they drink some water.

2   Against their tummy – their belly or abdomen.

3   Against their lower chest on the left side.

4   Now put a seashell or cup over their ear and listen.

- The noise you hear when you listen to a heartbeat is the sound of the heart valve slapping shut. Your heart is in the middle of your chest; but the bottom tip touches the chest wall, on your left.

- When your tummy rumbles, you can hear gas bubbling through your guts. The gas is made by gut bacteria, digesting your food. Bacteria get more to digest from beans and other vegetables; so these foods make more gas.

- The noise you hear when you put a seashell to your ear sounds like the sea; but it is the blood swishing through the blood vessels of your ear flap.

- Squishing sounds from your belly are from food being pushed through your gut – like toothpaste along a tube.

Presentation

Students could use PowerPoint to prepare a presentation on how the digestive system works. They might be able to incorporate images and video clips they find on the Internet to make their presentation more exciting.

At home   WS 14 WS 15

Ask students to record their eating for a week. How could they improve their diet themselves?

Ask students to complete WS 14 and WS 15, possibly as homework.

Plenary

Go back to the body organ maps and draw them again – this time with their enhanced knowledge. Admit that this is an unfair activity – the body organs overlap each other and are almost impossible to show in 2-D.

Unit 3: Humans – Organization

The objectives for this lesson are that students should be able to:

- Understand how each organ is important for life and that they cannot live without them

- Explain, using scientific terms, how the heart, lungs and digestive systems work

- Find out about the function of your heart in keeping you alive

- Find out more about what blood groups are and what their own blood group is.

SB pp.32–33
Starter

- Discuss how you would manage without some organs.

- *What would be the effect of losing your stomach, your lungs, your heart, your brain?*

- *Why does the body need these to function?*

- See the Science background for answers.

Explain

Systems

For good reasons, we separate the body systems and their functions to understand and teach about them. But they are all integral to our health and welfare. Some body organs have a variety of unrelated functions – the liver, for example. The liver has both regulatory and storage functions. It is the largest single organ in the body, weighing about 1.5 kg in an adult. It breaks down fats and breaks down waste products to urea, excreted by the kidneys. But it also makes essential vitamins and removes damaged blood cells and toxins from the blood.

Systems work together

The process of respiration breaks down our food to release energy. More than one system is involved in this process. The digestive system breaks down the food; the respiratory system provides the necessary oxygen – and removes the waste carbon dioxide. The blood system distributes the food and oxygen to the cells, and removes the waste products. Actual respiration takes place in all the cells of the body, in tiny organelles inside every cell, called mitochondria. Without the body

systems, the cells would be starved of the raw materials of respiration.

Waste disposal

Children have a natural fascination with their excretory functions. Humans produce several kinds of waste. The most familiar are faeces – which are the remains of food, micro-organisms and some body products including bile – and urine, which contains excess water and waste products in the form of the yellow pigment urea. But gas exchange in the lungs (sometimes wrongly called respiration) also releases waste carbon dioxide, and some water is also lost from our skins as sweat.

Things to do

Heartbeat

Explore, objectively, changes to the body after exercise. Measure the change in heart rate and the pulse, and compare this before and after exercise. Offer some explanations as to why this should be – greater need for energy, greater amounts of waste products produced.

Students have difficulty finding their pulse. They can use their fingertips – not their thumb, which has a pulse of its own – in the small valley at the base of their hand. Or they can feel a pulse on their temples close to the hairline; or without pressing, in their necks.

Skip through the heart

You can draw a heart on the playground and play a hopping game through it, the students hopping in from the body, out to the lungs, back to the heart again and finally off to the body once more. Are they hopping into the correct side of the heart? Are they carrying lots of oxygen – or lots of carbon dioxide?

Record

Groups might adopt a body system and find out all they can about it. Then they can share their information with others through a short presentation.

Support

Students can be helped to understand the relationships of the body organs to one another by modelling the internal organs and putting them together.

Extend

Some body systems can be represented through drama. Students have drawn a blood system on the ground and moved through it as blood cells, or become 'food' and moved through hoops representing parts of the digestive system.

Dig deeper

Revise their understanding of heart rate and exercise. Explore diet and activity and heart disease. Study the composition of the blood. Students could find out more about the heart, fitness and blood cells and how they work.

Did you know?

These are the principal organ systems of the human body:

Digestive – processing food from the stomach, intestines, etc;

Endocrine – communication around the body with hormones;

Excretory – getting rid of waste with kidneys and bladder;

Immune – defence against disease;

Integumentary – skin, hair and nails;

Muscular – muscles and movement;

Nervous – transferring information to and from the brain to make the body react;

Reproductive – sexual organs;

Respiratory – lungs and diaphragm;

Skeletal – bones ligaments and tendons.

Many students may not realize that plants have organs too. They obviously aren't the same as mammals. These include a transport system, which is similar to our circulatory system but without a heart; a reproductive system that is the flower, ovary, etc. and a vegetative system, which is the root, stem and leaves.

I wonder...

If an organ or organ system fails to work properly then you will become ill. It depends on the organ and the system as to how ill you become. If a kidney stops working, then you can continue an almost normal life, as you have two kidneys and your body can function with just one. If your heart stops working completely this is fatal. However

some people have a heart defect, e.g. a hole in the heart. They can still live a relatively normal life, but may not be able to exercise much as the blood carrying the oxygen isn't being pumped as efficiently as it should be.

Other ideas

Investigate students' basic understanding of their circulatory system. *Where is your heart? Where does your blood go?* Question the idea that the body is a 'bag of blood'. You might ask students to draw their idea of the circulatory system, and compare it with the correct picture – that there are tubes and a central pump.

Explore, subjectively, changes in the circulation with exercise – faster heart rate, skin flushing, thumping pulse. Ask the students to record the changes in themselves with exercise. They could draw themselves twice – once before and one after exercise – recording differences in how they look and feel.

How should you deal with small cuts and scrapes? Why? Talk about hygiene and health.

Presentation

A number of digital resources offer animations of the heart pumping and blood circulating. Use these to explore in this format the way the blood circulates.

At home

Ask students to find out what a blood group is, and their own grouping. *Does anyone in your family donate blood? What is it used for? Has anyone received a transfusion?* (Be alert to sensitivities; some cultures and religious groups forbid blood transfusion.)

Ask students to complete WS 16 as homework to reinforce their learning.

Plenary

Students could present their findings as annotated pictures, or use ICT to show the stages in the beating of the heart and the flow of blood. There are models available that show the flow of blood through the heart. Ask them to devise some basic health rules for a healthy heart.

Unit 3: Humans – Digestion

The objectives for this lesson are that students should be able to:

- Explore how the digestive system is essential to all animals and how it works

- Explain the processes of the digestive system

- Find out about foods that aid digestion

- Keep a record of foods they eat and consider how to improve their diets.

SB pp.34–35

Starter

- Bring in a plate of food. This could be any of a number of possibilities – a meal left from school lunch, a 'healthy' meal, an ethnic meal or one eaten by a family in a famine-hit country, for example. Or one related to your current work in geography or history. Use the meal to discuss dietary needs, appropriately for your class.

Discuss whether food looks like this when it has been chewed. The food has to be broken down to get the nutrients from it.

This can lead to discussion on waste products, which students may find either fascinating or revolting. Treat it as a fact of life. Point out that every living organism has to pass waste out of its body.

Explain

The long journey

Your food has a lengthy journey ahead of it. It may be inside your gut for 30 hours, and be squirted with 17 different chemicals. Your digestive systems is the place where food is broken down into a state to go into the bloodstream.

Munching and mashing

It all takes place below the heart and lungs in your tummy – or more correctly, your abdomen. Here, the chewed food is thoroughly mixed up with chemicals that help to dissolve it. Your stomach can hold about as much gunge as a large pop bottle – around two litres.

Squirting and splashing

It takes about two to four hours to turn your meal into a thick soup that is squirted into your small intestine. The first part of this journey is through a 30 cm length called the duodenum, where digestive juices – enzymes from the pancreas, bile from the liver – are added. The bile squirts in like washing-up liquid.

Through the rest of the 6.5 metres of the 2.5 cm wide small intestine, the food is absorbed into the bloodstream ready for your body to use. The velvety lining of the small intestine, with its villi 'fingers', acts like blotting paper, soaking up all the useful materials and passing a thick pasty sludge into the large intestine.

The shorter (1.8 metre), thicker (7.5 cm) large intestine is full of harmless bacteria that help break down the rest of the food so that the body can use the water and minerals. The remaining food waste – coloured brown by pigments from the bile – begins to pile up behind the anus, waiting for you to go to the lavatory.

Your food is pushed along on its journey by waves of muscular squeezes. These work so well that you can eat and swallow when you are upside down – or in weightless conditions in space.

Things to do

How long is your intestine?

Model the digestive system from recycled materials, using a large box as the trunk, a plastic bottle for the stomach and plastic tube for the gut. Using the rope or tubing to make the intestines; then placing them in a box illustrates how long they are.

Moving food

The process by which you can squeeze toothpaste from the tube is similar to peristalsis in the gut. The gut works by squeezing behind the food and then pushing it forwards. Explore the best way to move the 'food' (toothpaste) fastest or to get the most out in one go. This can be messy but fun!

Record

Students could record their food's journey through the gut – 'I'm your breakfast, and this is what happens to me!'

Support

Encourage the use of the correct terminology – 'stomach' rather than 'tummy', for example, which will help when interpreting illustrations.

Extend

Ask students to find out more about dietary fibre or roughage – the undigested plant material that adds bulk to the gut contents and aids digestion.

Dig deeper

Students could find out more about digestion. They could also research the liver and pancreas.

Did you know?

The muscle movements are called peristalsis. A ball or bolus of food is pushed ahead of each muscle wave.

I wonder...

This can be worked out as a maths problem, either by weighing the average meal and working it out, or by counting up the number of meals per day, then per year and seeing how much each meal would be.

Other ideas

Ask students to research and explain the functions of the main organs of the digestive system. Each student could take one organ, then the group could pool their research to give an idea of how the whole gut works.

Categorize the foods students eat as containers of carbohydrates, proteins, fats, vitamins and mineral salts. Ask students to record their intake of each and how balanced their diet is.

Where are their deficiencies? Where are their excesses? How could their diet be improved?

Devise a balanced diet that contains the main food groups. Compare that with the diet the students regularly eat. Suggest some ways that their choices of school meal would improve their diet.

Presentation

During your life, you will eat the equivalent weight of 14 adult elephants (without the tusks). You can expect to eat 80 000 meals, running your gut continuously for 650 000 hours. Ask students to present ideas like these in imaginative ways.

Ask the students to make 'stop wasting food' posters.

At home

WS 17

Ask the students to keep a food diary and categorize their foods.

WS 17 is a bit of fun. It makes a great, if messy, demonstration, or could be a science club activity. It models what happens to food in the stomach.

Plenary

Students are fascinated by faults in the digestive system – including sickness and diarrhoea! Use this to teach them more about food hygiene and sensible eating.

Your stomach will reject more than it can handle – or anything that irritates the stomach lining. If you stretch your stomach too far, it will tell your brain that it's in pain. This is stomach ache. The 'vomit centre' in the brain gets signals from your body – which include the signals it sends when you are standing at the back of a boat. If the signals are strong enough, they trigger a convulsion of your stomach muscles, and you are sick. The sour taste is from the acids working in your stomach.

Your stomach stops digesting if you are very frightened, preparing your body for the danger. You get 'butterflies' or cramps. Diarrhoea is a safety mechanism set off by food that irritates. Your gut pushes all its contents through in a rush, to prevent damage. Fibre is hardly digested at all. It fills your large intestine, pushing out food that has dried out and is hard to get rid of. Fibre-rich foods like brown rice and wholemeal bread help deal with constipation.

Unit 3: Humans – Breathing in and out

The objectives for this lesson are that students should be able to:

- Understand why the respiratory system is essential to all life

- Explain the processes of the respiratory system

- Understand that exercise makes them use their respiratory system differently

- Measure their fitness by counting their breathing after exercise.

SB pp.36–37 *Starter*

- Come in with a face mask and snorkel. Ask why you need the snorkel. Surely you can breathe underwater? You can't!

Explain

You need oxygen

The human body is unable to store oxygen.

We need oxygen every moment of the day. Even when sitting still, doing very little, we cannot stop the tick-over of our body systems. Our brain alone, even when we seem to be inactive, is whirring away, demanding energy. It is a high energy user. Our heads stay hot even when the rest of us is cold. The brain is continuing to control the body processes, shuffle and back up files, and all this activity produces heat. That's why wearing a hat keeps in so much of our body heat. We are covering a major heat generator.

Special sponges

Lungs are more like sponges than bags. We have two of them – one larger than the other – and they sit inside a protective cage of bones called the ribs. They inflate and deflate; and as they do so, they pull in and push out air. We call this breathing.

We can see that our chest gets bigger and smaller when we breathe; but this is not the only way that the lungs expand and contract. A muscular drumskin called the diaphragm shuts off the bottom of the chest cavity. This drumskin can contract, becoming flat – or relax, becoming domed. This change in shape makes the lung cavity bigger and smaller.

The chest cavity – the box containing the lungs – is sealed. If it gets bigger, it creates a vacuum inside it. If it gets smaller, it puts pressure on the lungs. Because they are open to the air through your nose, the lungs respond to their changes in pressure by getting bigger and smaller. The chest expands and the diaphragm flattens – the chest cavity gets bigger – the lungs expand – air rushes in. The chest gets smaller, the ribs press in, the diaphragm becomes domed – the lungs squash and air is pushed out. And all without the diaphragm or the ribs touching the lungs themselves.

In and out

If you are a tiny cell living contentedly in the middle of a belly button, how is this oxygen going to get to you? The answer is that it will have to go on a bit of a journey.

The first part of the journey is in through your mouth – or your nose – and down a stiff pipe called the trachea. This branches into two bronchi – one for each lung. Now the air travels down tunnels that get narrower and narrower, branching as they go. The thinner branches – the bronchioles – go on getting thinner until each reaches a handful of small bags – the alveoli. These look like a bunch of grapes – but these are thin-walled hollow grapes with room inside each for a spoonful of air. And it is through these that the gases are exchanged and the oxygen enters the blood stream.

That may not seem like much oxygen; but there are thousands upon thousands of alveoli – so many that someone has calculated that – spread out – they would cover a complete tennis court.

In each grape – each alveolus – an exchange takes place. Oxygen-rich air in – carbon dioxide-rich air out. Not that all the oxygen is absorbed, nor is all the gas breathed out carbon dioxide. The air you breathe out is different from the air you breathed in. Less oxygen; more carbon dioxide.

And the oxygen you've taken in? Well, that gets whipped away by the blood system and eventually arrives at that lonely cell in the belly button, where it is welcomed to help that cell respire.

Things to do

Do you breathe through your nose?

Ask students to follow the activity in the *Student Book*. Feathers can work better than tissues, but can make students sneeze.

What's in the air we breathe?

This activity links to not only finding out what the different gases are in the air, but also to the transmission of diseases. Abu-Ali al-Husayn ibn Abdullah ibn-Sina, known as Ibn Sina or Avicenna, was a Persian philosopher and physician who observed transmission of infectious diseases through the air. He also wrote a book called the 'Canon of Medicine' which was a complete summary of Islamic medicine at that time. It formed the basis of medical study in European universities and medical schools from the 12th to the 18th centuries.

Did you know?

- You take around 600 million breaths in your life, taking in about six litres of air every minute. Average resting breathing is 15–17 breaths a minute. You may take 80 breaths a minute during vigorous exercise. New-born babies breathe 40 times a minute.

- There are 300 million alveoli in your lungs. You breathe about 15 cubic metres of air a day – enough to fill a small room or six phone boxes.

I wonder...

Most fishes can't breathe air, and mammals like us can't breathe underwater. A whale is a mammal, and it can't breathe underwater either. It will dive to a considerable depth, taking with it the oxygen it needs for around half an hour of activity before coming to the surface again, blowing off the carbon dioxide it has accumulated, taking in great draughts of oxygen and diving again.

Other ideas

The breath of life

Ask students to talk about their breathing and how it varies in different circumstances. We breathe deeply when exercising. We take deep breaths when swimming – but not underwater. We take a deep breath before diving or jumping in. Establish that we need air to live, and that we cannot breathe underwater.

How fit are you?

Emphasize that speed of recovery is only one measure of fitness. There are others. Do not put pressure on (as in any physical activity) students who suffer with asthma or breathing problems.

Short of breath

Ask student to do different activities and record the changes in their breathing; but note that breathing is directly under our control and that they can voluntarily take more – or fewer – breaths than they need. Discuss their subjective discoveries. When do we breathe faster – and slower. What do we mean when we say 'out of breath'? Why do we take deep breaths when we are frightened? Is it to prepare us for fight or flight? Why does excitement leave us 'breathless'?

Presentation

Ask students to prepare a presentation on the importance of clean air.

At home

WS 18

Ask students to record activities that had them breathing deeply. What did they have in common? Ask students to complete WS 18 as homework.

Plenary

Students can understand the function of the lungs by modelling the chest cavity.

Cut the base off a small plastic bottle (the chest). Plug the neck with plasticine and push a small tube through the it (the trachea) that has a balloon (the lungs) tightly fixed to the end. Close the base of the bottle tightly with a sheet of burst balloon (the diaphragm). Pull the centre of the diaphragm. This reduces the pressure in the chest and the lung should expand. Release the diaphragm and the lungs will return to normal. Discuss why a puncture of the chest can lead to a lung collapsing. Point out that this is why the chest is so well protected with a cage of ribs.

Unit 3: Humans – Dealing with waste/Controlling your body

The objectives for this lesson are that students should be able to:

- Recognise that humans produce waste.

- Recall that waste gases are lost through the lungs.

- Learn that waste water and other materials are excreted by the kidneys

- Understand that your nervous system is your brain and nerves.

- Learn that your nervous system controls what your body does.

SB pp.38–39 **Starter**

- TThere are two different topics in this lesson – kidneys and excretion, and the nervous system. Split them to save confusion, but emphasise that both systems are essential to the effective functioning of the body.

- There may be some embarrassment or jokes at the mention of some body functions. You will handle this in your own way, but emphasize the importance of these systems for our survival. In a hot country, dehydration is a threat, and it is only common sense for students to understand, for example, that their urine should be pale yellow ('straw-coloured' most books say) and that if it is darker, they need to drink more.

- Toilet visits are a routine part of a primary school day. But you could start by questioning why they are necessary. *Why do we go to the toilet? What are we losing?* And linking to the nervous system: *How do we know we need to go? And what tells our bodies we are in the toilet?*

- Our bladders (and lungs) are under our control – unlike our intestines and heart.

Explain

Kidneys

The blood system is the body's main means of transport. Blood carries nutrients and oxygen to each and every cell, and takes away the waste products. Like room service in a hotel with a billion rooms, the blood system sees that each cell gets the attention it needs.

Your kidneys are at the base of your back. They are two important organs, each the size of a fist. They control the amount of water in your body, filtering your blood and letting waste products through so that you can lose them in the lavatory. They hold back the salts essential to a healthy life.

If one of your kidneys were to fail, the other would grow bigger and take over the work of the missing kidney. People who have lost both kidneys can have a new one transplanted from someone else. Relatives and some friends can donate a kidney. They can go on living with just one.

Nervous system

Your nervous system has many tiny neurons. Each neuron has a body with fine hairs or dendrites. The dendrites pick up messages from the sense organs. Each nerve cell has one or more long axons. Nerve messages travel along the axons, connecting the neurons together. The neurons may receive messages, or send them. The messages travel at about 400 km an hour, so you only take a fraction of a second to react to things.

Striped body muscles are under our conscious control and their ends are usually attached by tendons to bones. Smooth muscles are controlled by the autonomic nervous system and are in the gut, blood vessels, and various ducts. Cardiac muscle is present only in the heart, and is also controlled by the autonomic nervous system, too. The autonomic nervous system functions without our being conscious of it.

Some students will have apparent sensory difficulties – impaired hearing, short sight – and others may have less obvious problems, such as colour blindness, a poor sense of smell or taste. Recent research has shown that the number of taste buds per square centimetre of tongue can vary in individuals from tens to thousands.

Things to do

Giving life

The kidneys are one part of the body that can be given to others. Kidney patients and others may welcome a transplant: the donation of body parts from living or dead people.

It is currently possible to transplant:

- Blood – Many people are blood donors. It can be used to replace lost blood.

- Bone marrow – This is taken from living people to help patients with illnesses.

- The cornea – This is the 'window' of the eye. It can cloud over with age.

- Kidneys – These remove waste products from the body. People can survive with one.

- The heart – Pumps blood round the body.

- Lungs – The lungs collect the oxygen and lose carbon dioxide waste.

- The liver – An important organ in very many ways.

Other ideas

There are a great many activities possible to explore the senses and nervous system. Choose from these:

- Our eyes give us more information than the rest of our senses put together. This is well-illustrated by blindfolding students and asking them to identify some sounds, made with percussion instruments, for example.

- Our external ears collect sounds and direct them into our ears. Simple paper cones will demonstrate how sounds can be collected and identified. The cones should not come to a point – cut off any points – and must not be put into ears.

- A scented air freshener is a great demonstration of both our sense of smell and how gases fill a room. Ask the students to raise their hands when they can smell the freshener, and you will see hands raised one by one as the scent fills the classroom.

- Our senses of smell and taste are very closely related. Blindfolded, and without a sense of smell (hold your nose) it is hard to tell potato, apple and carrot slices apart when tasting them.

- Different parts of our bodies are more or less sensitive to touch. Round-ended hairpins are an ideal testing tool. You can feel two separate touches on the fingertips, but only one on the small of the back.

- Many of our body movements are voluntary – that is to say they are controlled by our conscious thoughts. But others are involuntary or autonomic. Ask students to investigate the autonomic reaction of the iris to light. Students can work in pairs, but warn them in advance not to shine bright lights directly into each other's eyes. If one student closes his/her eyes while the other watches closely, the moment the eyes open, the iris can be seen closing down. Similarly, if the student is in dark or shady conditions and the light is shone towards his/her eye – but not directly into it – the iris contracts to reduce the amount of light.

Did you know?

Nervous impulses through huge animals like some dinosaurs needed a further push when they had passed through their bodies. A nerve plexus at the base of the tail boosted the message. It was not – as some might believe – a second brain.

I wonder...

Animals are unable to make their own food; because of that, they have had to develop ways of moving to food sources. Once a living thing moves, it needs sense organs to find its way around. Putting the sense organs at the front or top of the body makes them more useful.

If the animal is a secondary consumer – a predator or carnivore – the sense organs are likely to be forward-facing, enabling it to see its prey and to catch it efficiently. If the animal is a primary consumer or herbivore, then its sense organs are likely to survey the surroundings more generally, because it needs to be aware of predators and danger. Cats have eyes on the front of their heads; mice have them on the side. Cats have excellent, stereoscopic forward vision to catch mice; mice have good all-round vision to spot and avoid cats.

Plenary

Ask students to draw a flow chart of the steps that take place when they take a certain action. For example, how do their brain, nervous system, muscle system and skeleton work together to enable them to pick up a glass and drink? What senses do they use? How important are their eyes and sense of touch?

Some people are born with or suffer from some sensory problems. How do they cope without certain senses or with them severely impaired? In what ways can we restore the senses or improve their sensory abilities?

Unit 3: Humans – Unit 3: Review

The objectives for this lesson are that students should be able to:

- Check what they have learned about humans in this unit

- Find out how they are working towards, within and beyond the Grade 6 level.

SB p.40 **Expectations**

Students working towards Grade 6 will:

- recognize that humans are animals and that we are all alive

- state the 7 processes of life

- name some of the major organs in the body and their positions.

In addition, students working within Grade 6 will:

- recognize that the body is made up of many different organs, with different jobs to do

- describe some of the functions of these organs and how they are essential to life

- describe how some of these organs work together in a system

- recognize that all mammals have similar organs and organ systems

- describe some of the same basic requirements that animals have, although they may have different ways of doing this

- collect evidence from a variety of sources and present this clearly to back up their claims.

Further to this, students working beyond Grade 6 will also:

- debate about organ donation and consider the merits or not of animal experimentation

- recognize that some ideas are difficult to test.

Check-up

The brain uses around one-ninth of the body's energy needs, and of course it never stops working even when we are asleep. Such activity produces heat and, in cold conditions, wearing a hat can prevent considerable heat loss.

Assessment WS 19 WS 20

Use the Unit 3 assessment on WS 19 and WS 20 to check the students' understanding of the content of the unit. The answers are given opposite.

Name: _____ Date: _____

WS 19 Unit 3 assessment 1

1 Name the body organs that:
   a) pump air around the body _____
   b) fill with air when we breathe _____
   c) fill with food from our mouths when we eat _____

2 Which two organs are in your chest? _____ and _____

3 Which system:
   a) carries blood around your body? _____
   b) changes the food in your body? _____
   c) exchanges carbon dioxide for oxygen? _____

4 Join the words with arrows to show how your blood circulates. You will need one word twice.

heart	lungs	body

Unit 3: Humans   19

Unit 3 assessment 2 (WS 20)

Name: _____   **Date:** _____

5 What are the correct words for:

a) the small bags inside your lungs? _____

b) the muscular sheet that helps you breathe? _____

c) the tube from your mouth to your stomach? _____

d) the pressure wave of blood from your heart? _____

e) the muscular bag where your food is churned up?

_____

6 a) How does the oxygen get from the air to the cells of your body?

_____

_____

_____

_____

b) How does carbon dioxide from your cells get into the air?

_____

_____

_____

_____

20   Heinemann Explore Science Grade 6

2 heart and lungs

3 **a** blood or circulatory

   b digestive

   c respiratory

4 Starting at any point: heart > lungs > heart > body

5 **a** alveoli

   b diaphragm

   c oesophagus or esophagus

   d pulse

   e stomach

6 **a** Variations on: air > lungs > blood > cells

   b Variations on: cells > blood > lungs > air

The answer!

The Unit begins with Ahmed wondering why his heart beats faster and he breathes harder with exercise. Students should now understand that this is because he needs to release extra energy. More exercise demands more oxygen and produces more carbon dioxide, so greater activity is required by the heart and lungs.

And finally...

A visit to an interactive centre featuring the human body would round off this Unit perfectly.

Answers

1 **a** heart

   b lungs

   c stomach

Unit 4: More about dissolving

The objectives for this Unit are that students should be able to:

- Separate insoluble and soluble solids from liquids

- Plot accurate charts and graphs of their results

- Discover how to make water pure

- Measure volumes of liquid.

SB p.41   *Science background*

When a solid dissolves in a liquid, the particles of solid are evenly distributed among the liquid particles. Once the liquid is unable to hold any more solid particles the solutions is said to be saturated, just as a piece of fabric is saturated when it can't hold any more water. This is when you start to see the solid in the solution, usually as particles at the bottom of the vessel. The amount of solid that will dissolve in a liquid is dependent on:

- the size of the particles of solid, i.e. the bigger and heavier the particles, the less solid that the liquid can dissolve

- the temperature of the liquid, i.e. the more energy the particles in the liquid have, the faster they are moving and the more solid particles they can hold up, similar to a juggler keeping more objects in the air if they are moving faster

- the type of liquid the solid is in.

For primary students the liquid is almost always water. Water is a solvent. Other familiar solvents include acetone (nail varnish remover) and alcohol. The solid dissolving in the solvent is called the solute. It's not necessary for students to be familiar with these words at this level; solid and liquid are acceptable.

The speed at which a solid dissolves depends on the energy of the liquid particles. If you heat them, they have more energy, so move faster and pick up the solid particles faster. If you stir the liquid, you give the liquid particles more movement energy and the solid dissolves faster.

When a solution starts to evaporate, only the liquid particles can escape from the solution. The liquid particles are smaller than the solid particles and need less energy to escape from the solution. This is why the solid is left behind. The liquid leaving the solution is pure. This is the basis behind the principle of evaporation.

Language

Condense	To turn from a gas back into a liquid. This normally happens when the gas is cooled or meets a cool surface.
Decant	To pour a liquid off from the top of an undissolved solid.
Dissolve	A solid 'disappears' into a liquid. The particles of solid are evenly distributed between the liquid particles.
Evaporate	A liquid becomes a gas at a temperature below its boiling point. The particles on the surface of the liquid gain enough energy from the surroundings to escape the liquid and become a vapour.
Insoluble	A solid that doesn't dissolve in a liquid.
Mixture	Two substances in contact with each other that are not joined or dissolved, so they can be separated.
Pure	A single substance.
Saturated	A solution in which no more solid will dissolve.
Solution	A solid dissolved in a liquid.
Temperature	A measurement of how hot or cold something is.
Thermometer	A device for measuring temperature.

The Words to learn list on page 41 of the *Student Book* can be used to make a classroom display.

Resources

- *Material Changes* Reader
- A selection of plastic cups
- Some cotton wool
- Dirty water, with gravel and mud in it
- A sample of clean sand
- A sample of salty water
- A kettle
- Petri dishes
- Thermometers

- Measuring cylinders
- Several scoops, e.g. those used to measure a teaspoon in the kitchen, or teaspoons
- Samples of sugar, salt, chalk, talcum powder, sand, bicarbonate of soda, sherbet, baking powder, bath salts.

Bright ideas

Ask children for analogies of dissolving and saturation. For example, an empty football stadium is rather like a liquid solvent; people entering are like the solid solute. They fill the seats in the stadium. When the stadium is full, it is 'saturated' – it cannot take any more solid.

Knowledge check

Students should have practised measuring volume and temperature in previous years and are consolidating this knowledge in this unit. Although the theory of how solids dissolve is not required, students should know that not all solids dissolve in water. They will have discovered that the solids that don't dissolve can be filtered from a liquid, or even sieved if the solid pieces are very large. Students may have seen this kind of separation in everyday life when using coffee filters and tea bags.

Skills check

Student needs to:

- measure volume accurately
- measure temperature accurately
- be able to draw a bar chart.

Some students will:

- present results on a line graph
- explain why measurements need to be repeated.

Links to other subjects

Literacy: Reading and following simple instructions, e.g. how long it takes sugar to dissolve and how many sugars can be dissolved in tea.

Numeracy: Reading scales, e.g. thermometers and measuring cylinders. Using stopwatches. Presenting data in the form of line graphs.

ICT: Using a temperature sensor. Using a multimedia package to combine text and graphs to make a presentation.

Let's find out...

The Unit opens with this question:

If you are making instant flavoured noodles, do you put the water or the noodles in the bowl first? What happens to the powder? What temperature of water do you start with? How can you cook the noodles faster? Before you eat the noodles, you have to leave them for a few minutes. Why? And what happens to all the vegetables in the noodles? Why don't they disappear when the water is added?

Unit 4: More about dissolving – Filtering and sieving

The objectives for this lesson are that students should be able to:

- Find out whether all solids dissolve in water
- Learn how to separate insoluble solids from water by filtering
- Make predictions on how to make clean water
- Research ways of separating solids from liquids.

SB pp.42–43 **Starter**

- Show a filter, a sieve and a colander. Discuss how each is used to separate solids from liquids. Why would you not use a colander for sieving lumps from flour? Discuss the properties of different solids and liquids.

- Write the words solid and liquid on the board, dividing the board in two. Ask the students what words or ideas or examples they can think of for each term. This should elucidate their understanding of the main properties.

Explain   WS 21

Separating solids from liquids...

Give the students a range of solids, powder and lumps to add to water. Recap that some solids dissolve and some don't. A table could be drawn up by the students – see if they can design it themselves – to predict and show the results.

Separate ways

Sieve some marbles or dried peas and water, then try fine sand and water. Ask the students what is happening (the sand particles are so small that they go through the holes in the sieve). Ask the students how you can alter the sieve to ensure the sand doesn't go through.

You can show the students how a sieve works by using an acetate (OHP) sheet and making holes in it with a compass point. Put sand and water on it. The sand doesn't go through. It you make the holes bigger then the sand starts to go through. This shows that the size of the holes determines the size of the particles that go through.

Show a range of filters, e.g. tea bags, coffee percolators and cafetiéres, and discuss how they work. Students should complete WS 21.

Things to do

Water, water...

Show the students the first aid kit, which should include:

- cotton wool
- plasters
- safety pins
- gauze.

You also need to provide sand, small stones, a beaker of muddy water, a plastic cup and a clear glass beaker.

Make a filter by piercing the bottom of the plastic cup with a safety pin. Cotton wool should be placed in the bottom of the cup, followed by a layer of sand, and then a layer of small stones. The students can then pour the muddy water into the filter, collecting the resulting clear water in the glass beaker.

⚠ Students must not drink the water because materials may be dissolved in it.

Support

Some students will not know in which order to use the filters. Allow them to look at the cotton wool under a hand lens and judge whether it will allow small or large particles to go through. Encourage them to think logically: the sieves need to get finer as the water progresses through the filter.

Extend

All students should be able to produce a cleaner sample of water than they started with.

Some students could investigate how many times you need to pass the water through the homemade filter to get it really clear. They could also try different ways of filtering the muddy water.

Record

The students can draw a labelled diagram of their homemade filter, describing how it works. This could be turned into a display that can be added to, as there are other activities that lend themselves to this activity.

Dig deeper

An air filter is used in an internal combustion engine. It removes the impurities in the air before they mix with the fuel, just as our nose prevents impurities entering our lungs. There are other filters in a car too, filtering the fuel and the oil.

Did you know?

Humans have filters in their nose and throat. Fish have filters to protect their gills from clogging. The gills absorb the dissolved oxygen from water so they can respire under water.

I wonder...

Water can be filtered or sieved to get rid of larger particles, but the organisms that cause illnesses are far too small to be removed by this method. Try this with water and sand mixed. The water will still be coloured – showing that not everything has been removed. Or try filtering water with food colouring in it. It will still be coloured!

Other ideas

Other filters

Set the students a design and technology task to make their own filter. They can investigate with different materials, discovering why paper is a good material for a filter. They could also investigate the best paper towel to use as a filter, looking at its fibres under a microscope, and seeing how much water goes through before it is unusable.

The students could also examine filter papers under the microscope and observe the size of the holes related to the job of the filter. Include looking at sieves and compare them to a filter.

Presentation

You could do some role play to show how a filter works, which the students can use to do a presentation. You need to have a few students who will be the filter, to stand in a line with a space between each student. The other students are the solid particles. They can either be single students to show how small particles, like sand, pass through the filter holes, or large particles represented by two or three students with arms linked. These groups of students can't get through the filter holes but if the filter holes are made bigger, i.e. the filter students are spread out, then they will be able to get through the holes.

At home

Ask the students to look at home for examples of filters being used, e.g. plug holes, coffee filters, tea bags, dishwashers and tumble driers.

Plenary

Show a range of filters, and sieves, e.g. colanders, kitchen sieves, soil sieves, coffee filters, tea bags, muslin. Discuss the size of particle that can go through each of these and the reason why each filter is used.

Unit 4: More about dissolving – Separating solids and liquids

The objectives for this lesson are that students should be able to:

- Understand what a solution is

- Find out whether they can remove a solid from a solution by filtering

- Research what happens to a solution when the water evaporates

- Explain the results of their evaporation experiments.

SB pp.44–45

Starter

- Show a range of liquids, of which some have soluble solids in them. You could use water with food colours, inky water, salt water, distilled water, sandy water, floury water. Ask the students to guess which are solutions.

- Once the students have decided which are the solutions, ask them if the solutions are pure or not. Discuss the meaning of 'pure', i.e. made of only one substance that can't be separated.

- Show a picture of vitamin or indigestion tablets dissolving in water (or demonstrate the real thing). Ask the students to explain what is happening.

Explain

What's the answer?

Care needs to be taken here with the use of language, because solution is not only used in science for a solid that has dissolved in a liquid, but also in maths for the answer to a problem.

Which to remove?

Show that a solution goes straight through a filter without leaving anything behind in the filter. Discuss with the students how you could get rid of the water. They did this in Grade 4, so recap the principles of evaporation.

The Father of Chemistry

Jabir ibn Hayyan is credited with being the Father of Chemistry. Robert Boyle is called the father of modern chemistry, building on more ancient work.

During his time, Jabir, also known as Geber, would have been known as an alchemist looking for the elixir of life and the philosophers' stone to turn metals into gold. However, he not only described crystallization, but also distillation. He also designed pieces of laboratory equipment that are still in use today, like the retort stand. Much of his work formed the basis of modern chemistry.

Things to do

Going, going, gone

The students put Petri dishes or saucers of substances in a warm place to observe the effects of evaporation. Use a range of solutions such as lemonade, inky water, salt water, sugar water, distilled water, etc. The activity asks the students how they will keep the investigation fair. They will need to measure the volume of the solution to start with, and put all the saucers in the same place for the same length of time.

Support

By only using small amounts of liquid the evaporation time will be reduced, so the students will see the results more quickly and their interest will be retained. Putting the solutions in a shallow dish rather than a deep one will aid evaporation.

Extend

All students should be able to observe that when a solution is left in a warm place the water 'disappears' leaving the solid that was dissolved in the bottom of the vessel. This is called the residue, because it 'resides' or lives in the bottom of the vessel.

Some students will be able to explain, with the aid of diagrams, what has happened to the water. They could then investigate whether the size and shape of the vessel holding the solution alters the length of time for the water to evaporate.

Another group of students could weigh the amount of solid added to the liquid, then weigh the amount of solid retrieved from the solution after the water has evaporated. This shows that none of the solid is lost during evaporation, only the liquid.

Record

The information gained from the investigation can be recorded in the form of annotated diagrams that show where the water goes and the conditions needed for the water to evaporate.

If you have a video camera, set it to take time-lapse pictures of the dishes and the water evaporating.

Dig deeper

A solute is the solid that is being dissolved into the liquid. The solvent is the liquid that dissolves the solute. The solvent doesn't have to be water. It is the most common solvent that the students will meet.

Did you know?

Both are examples of evaporation in everyday life.

I wonder...

Obviously you could leave rice and water to evaporate so the rice is left dry, but it would be quicker to filter or sieve the rice and water. You could set up the two investigations and explore which is quicker and which produces the driest rice. You might find that a combination of the two dries the rice fastest.

Other ideas

Keep it

Ask the students to design a device in design and technology that will stop evaporation from happening. This will normally involve placing a lid on the vessel containing the solution, but the students may have some other ideas. They can investigate whether the shape of the vessel (long and tall or shallow and wide) affects evaporation.

Opaque solutions

Challenge the students to make a solution that is not transparent. If the solid doesn't dissolve then it is not a solution. Remind students that a solution can be coloured, but also transparent. Incidentally, milk is not a solution, but a colloid. 'Colloid' is the scientific term for a mixture, e.g. fat droplets in water (milk). Smoke, aerosols and shaving foam are all colloids.

Crystals

When a solution evaporates it leaves behind the solid. Sometimes the solid forms crystals if the liquid is left to evaporate very slowly. Even sugar solution will produce crystals that can be seen. Make a saturated solution, (one where no more solid will dissolve) with something like sugar, salt or alum (from the chemist). Place a shallow dish of the solution in a warm place with a cotton thread lying in it, the ends overhanging the edges of the dish. Crystals should form on the thread. You could challenge the students to see who can produce the biggest crystal and how they did it. If you place the dish (preferably a Petri dish) of the solution under a digital microscope with a time lapse or camera facility, then the crystals could be observed growing. The crystals should have quite defined edges. Crystals start to grow around imperfections such as specks of dust. To avoid having lots of crystals growing all through the dish make sure the dish is clean and kept covered. Then the crystals will form on the thread.

Presentation

Take time-lapse pictures of the solution evaporating. These could be used, run at a faster speed, in a PowerPoint presentation to show what happens when you remove the water from a solution and showing the recovery of the solid. If you grew crystals, time-lapse pictures could show the crystal enlarging as the water evaporates.

At home

WS 22

What examples of everyday evaporation can students find, e.g. washing on a line or in a tumble drier, washing-up left to dry, boiling sauces to make them thicker?

Ask students to complete WS 22.

Plenary

Ask the students to draw a cartoon to illustrate what happens to the water as it evaporates, leaving the solid behind in the vessel. This will help establish that the water goes into the air and doesn't 'disappear'.

Unit 4: More about dissolving – Making water pure

The objectives for this lesson are that students should be able to:

- Discover and explain how to make water pure

- Learn what happens to water when it becomes pure

- Understand what evaporates from a solution

- Draw a labelled diagram of their experiments.

SB pp.46–47

Starter

- Bring in some ink and ask the students if they think it is pure ink. What would happen if you boiled it? Show a mixture of sand and water and ask the students what would happen if you boiled that. They should realize that the water will 'disappear' or evaporate, leaving the sand in the bottom. The sand particles are too heavy to evaporate into the air. They are too big and heavy to even dissolve in the water

- Ask the students what happens to the mirror when they have a hot bath or shower. What is on the mirror? Is it soapy?

Explain

Where does it go?

Demonstrate that only water leaves a solution when the solution is heated. Place a baking tray in the freezer the night before the lesson. This will provide a cool surface for the condensation of evaporated water.

Make some salty water and ask the students to taste the water to check that it is salty. After a thorough risk assessment heat the solution in a vessel, e.g. saucepan. You will need to make sure that the cold metal tray can be held at an angle of about 45° over the top of the saucepan to allow the steam to condense on it. At this angle the water droplets will run off the tray and you can collect them in a beaker. The collected water can be tested by the students to prove that the water is not salty.

⚠ The vessels used must be hygienic. It might be better to carry out these investigations in a kitchen or food technology room if possible, ensuring cleanliness is at a maximum, including the cold tray surface and the samples of salt or sugar.

Energy

You could demonstrate this with a role play. Ask all the students to group together as a solid. Draw a chalk line on the floor around them to represent the sides of a container, then tell them that only pupils/particles at the top can escape. Give some students a piece of paper to represent the heated particles and suggest that they move around and only leave the container if they reach the top part or mouth. Once they have left, they are a vapour and can move around more, but if they don't move away from the mouth of the container then the next particles can't leave.

Things to do

Should you drink seawater?

Discuss with the students how they could carry out an evaporation investigation using any items washed up on the shore. If there is time, they could set up the experiment. This might include a shallow vessel of salty water with a polythene bag over the top and sealed with a wire tie. If the set up is placed on a sunny window sill, the water will evaporate and then form droplets of pure water on the bag.

As it runs down it will make a pool of pure water around the bottom outside the vessel.

Humans cannot live on seawater because we are unable to excrete the amount of salt in it. It accumulates in our bodies, leading to chemical imbalance and eventual death.

Support

Some students will need help in planning the investigation. They may discover that the evaporated water will condense, even on surfaces that are not cold.

Extend

Some students could set up the investigation and leave it for several days. They could also try using salty water to see if they get the same results.

Record

Ask the students to draw a diagram of the apparatus with annotated labels that will remind them of what they did. This will also be a good way of assessing their learning so far, as diagrams and plans will show a misconception, or lack of understanding.

Dig deeper

The particles in a liquid gain energy from heat so they can move faster. They then start to escape the liquid and form a vapour. If a breeze is blowing then the vapour particles are removed from the liquid, so more evaporating particles can escape from the liquid.

Did you know?

Students could find out about air conditioning systems that remove heat through a change of state.

I wonder...

Soft drinks are a flavoured solution of water and sugar. If the students look at the ingredients list they should be able to make a prediction. If the main ingredient is water, then pure water could be extracted. What remains? Ingredients on food labels are listed with the main ingredient first.

Other ideas

Other liquids

The students could set up an investigation on evaporation using cola. They could then make predictions about other liquids, by looking at the relevant ingredients list. Some of the students could carry out further investigations using safe liquids. The results of the investigation form the basis of a table of results.

Water supply

The students could design and make a water recapture system to set up on an imaginary desert island.

Presentation

The role play of how a solution evaporates would provide an assembly presentation in front of the whole school (or a younger class).

The students could make a PowerPoint presentation to show that only the water leaves the solution. This could take the form of an 'evaporation movie' of several slides linked to show the process.

At home

WS 23

Ask the students to find out what happens if their parents or carers are cooking rice, for example, in a saucepan with the lid on compared with when the lid is left off. They could draw a labelled diagram to explain their observations. Alternatively, they could watch what happens when the kettle boils and the steam meets the wall.

Ask students to complete WS 23.

> ⚠ Remind the students that they must not touch the hot saucepans or the hot kettles themselves, only observe.

Plenary

Ask the students to produce a quick mind map of what they have learned about producing pure water from a solution. For example, start with the word 'solution' as the middle bubble and ask the students to suggest all the words associated with producing pure water.

Unit 4: More about dissolving – Dissolving jelly

The objectives for this lesson are that students should be able to:

- Discover how to dissolve jelly fast in different temperatures

- Make careful observations and record the changes they observe

- Display their results in a line graph

- Write instructions on how to dissolve jelly faster.

SB pp.48–49　Starter

- Discuss Sofia's problem of getting her jelly cubes to dissolve more quickly.

- Ask the students to think of other examples of dissolving in everyday life, such as sugar in tea. What can be done to a solution to make it dissolve faster?

- Ask the students how jelly is made at home. Families may use cubes or crystals; jellies may be started in the microwave oven (speeding up melting of the jelly, or heating the water with the jelly), or with boiling water (speeding up dissolving of the jelly in the water).

The challenge

Ask for ideas on ways to dissolve the jelly faster. These may include using hot water, stirring or using small pieces of jelly. Discuss how these all speed up dissolving. If anyone suggests heating the jelly cubes to melt them, explain the difference between melting and dissolving.

Read the opening of page 48 in the *Student Book*. Discuss how to make a jelly with the students. You could make up a jelly with them, to agree on when the jelly has all dissolved through discussion. Allow the children to taste the jelly and then give other ways in which they can tell the jelly is still in the water. This will reinforce that the jelly is still there, but not as a solid lump. As you make up the jelly, ask the students to think of all the ways they could make it dissolve faster.

Another advantage of making the jelly with them and setting the problem in a real context, is that you can ask the students to carefully observe the jelly as it dissolves, allowing them to see the way

the pieces get smaller and the jelly 'mixes' with the water, changing its colour.

What to do

The groups of students in the *Student Book* have decided to look at one aspect of what makes the jelly dissolve faster. You could set different groups of students off on different investigations, e.g. one to investigate temperature change, one to look at whether stirring is an issue, one to look at the size of the pieces and another group to look at the volume of water used.

What you need

- different coloured jelly cubes

- thermometers

- beakers, or clean plastic cups

- scissors

- stopwatches

- spoons, plastic ones are best

> ⚠ The jelly can only be eaten if it has been prepared in scrupulously hygienic conditions. This is unlikely to be the case. If you want to give the students a treat, make a jelly earlier yourself and this can be served at lunchtime. Be alert to cultural differences; some jellies are made with pork gelatine.

What to check

The students must agree on how many stirs to be performed in each investigation, e.g. 30 per minute. Also, they need to agree on a baseline temperature, e.g. 40 °C, size of jelly pieces, and the volume of water used.

> ⚠ The water for the investigation should only be hand-hot, not boiling from the kettle. You could demonstrate an investigation using close to boiling water.

Support

You will need to agree with the students how to tell if all the jelly has dissolved. These students could record their changes to the jelly in pictures or by taking photographs after each stir, or at timed intervals, that can be sequenced later. This will help with describing their observations.

Extend

Some students may be able to look at whether different types of jelly dissolve at different rates. More able students may consider what every parent knows – and that is to use as little hot water as possible and top up the final level with cold water, so it sets quickly!

More able students might realize that the temperature investigation isn't completely fair, as the water is cooling down as you are doing the investigation. As this happens in all the investigations at the same rate, as they are in the same room, this is still acceptable. Some students may want to change the jelly colour to see if this makes a difference. It can in practice.

What did you find? | WS 24

Record

The students could use the table provided on WS 24 to record their results. The data for all these investigations is continuous, so should be used to produce a line graph.

Alternatively, they could use the data given in the *Student Book*.

Present

The students could use the information they have pooled as a class to present the best way, scientifically, to dissolve jelly quickly. They could use the information to produce a list of instructions to be written on the back of a packet of jelly cubes.

Can you do better? | WS 25

Show the students Sofia's results on WS 25. Read it together. Is the reasoning behind her prediction correct? How do your results compare with hers? Would they tackle the investigation in a different way if they started again?

By making the pieces of jelly smaller, there is more surface area in contact with the water, so it dissolves faster and by stirring the solution the jelly is 'mixed' with the water faster.

Now predict

By stirring the tea and making sure it was hot to start with, the sugar would dissolve faster. The

students could also suggest that the sugar is added gradually, or make sure that grains are used, rather than sugar lumps.

Other ideas

Coffee break

Take a look at the time it takes for instant coffee to dissolve in different temperatures of water.

ICT ideas

Light sensor

One way of checking that all the jelly has dissolved is to place the beaker containing it on a transparent surface with a light sensor underneath. When all the jelly has dissolved the light sensor reading should go up.

Temperature sensor

The students could measure the temperature of the water with a temperature sensor to ensure they are accurate.

At home | WS 26

Ask the students to collect packets of foodstuffs from around the house. Then they can read the instructions on the backs of the packets looking for the ones that dissolve in water, e.g. instant soup, instant coffee. Look for instructions to stir, and to add hot water, and then look at the size of the particles in the packet. Then they can compare the results from their investigations with the instructions.

Ask students to complete WS 26.

Plenary

Show the students some effervescent indigestion tablets. If you were in a hurry, how could you make them dissolve faster? Show a whole tablet in water and time how long it takes to dissolve. Then try warmer water (not much effect), and then breaking it into smaller pieces.

Using Blu-tack, attach a piece of effervescent indigestion tablet to the inside of the lid of a camera film canister. Put a little water in the canister. Put the lid on. Invert the canister. Stand clear! How does water temperature affect the time and force of the 'pop'?

Unit 4: More about dissolving – Dissolving sugar

The objectives for this lesson are that students should be able to:

- Make predictions about what they think will happen

- Discover how much sugar will dissolve in different amounts of water

- Plan and carry out a fair test

- Explain why they need to repeat the measurements.

SB pp.50–51

Starter

- Discuss putting sugar in a hot drink. What would happen if you kept adding sugar? Would it keep dissolving? Would more or less sugar dissolve if the drink was cold?

The students may need to be introduced to the term 'saturated solution', but they may have already met 'saturated'. You could explain that a saturated solution is one that can't hold any more solid, whereas a saturated piece of fabric is one that can't hold any more water.

The challenge

Read the What to do and speech bubbles on page 50 in the *Student Book*. Discuss what happened at the beginning of the lesson with your cup of tea.

What to do

The first three comments made by the students are correct predictions, but the last one is something that your class could try, but actually makes no difference to the amount of sugar that will dissolve.

If you split the class into groups and give each group a different volume of water to work with, the class can then pool their results to produce a graph. Discuss with the students how to make their results more accurate. Explain that having more than one set of results means that they can check their results are correct. You could at this stage bring in the idea of taking an average of the results. It evens out the anomalous results.

What you need

- measuring cylinders
- sugar
- some teaspoons

What to check

The students will need to agree on how long to stir, so that all the investigations are fair. Stirring for 30 seconds would be fair. The temperature of the cold tap water should be constant; check with the thermometer.

Support

Some students may need help in checking when the sugar is dissolved. If there are a few grains left in the bottom of the beaker, then they can add another teaspoonful. If this doesn't dissolve, then the maximum number is the one before the last teaspoonful.

Extend

All students should be able to see that there is a maximum number of spoons of sugar that will dissolve. All students should see, when the class's results are pooled, that the more water they start with the more sugar will dissolve.

Some students could go on to investigate with water temperature and volume, or see if repeating the investigation makes any difference to the results.

What did you find?

WS 27

The students should use the table provided on WS 27 to record the total volume of water needed for the sugar to dissolve.

Record

The students can convert their recorded data into a graph. If the students are unable to produce their own data, they could use the students' data given in the *Student Book*. The data in this enquiry is continuous, as the more water you use the more sugar will dissolve.

Present

The line graph will show a trend to back up the prediction that the more water there is the more sugar will dissolve. Some students could use the graph and predict what will happen using higher volumes of water, or even draw a graph to show their prediction.

Can you do better?

WS 28

The students then decided to see if the type of sugar makes a difference to the dissolving time. Ask your students to complete the questions on WS 28. This worksheet could be done at home.

Now predict

Your class should be able to recognize that 80 ml of water will dissolve approximately 16 teaspoonfuls of sugar. It can be seen, even without the graph, that every 10 ml of water dissolves 2 teaspoonfuls of sugar.

Heating the water makes more sugar dissolve.

Other ideas

How much water?

The students could try finding the least amount of water needed to dissolve one teaspoonful of sugar.

ICT ideas

Light sensor

Once again, the light sensor could be used to see if there is any sugar that hasn't dissolved.

At home

The first stage in making instant soup is to add a small amount of water to the powder, but this will make the soup too thick. Has all the powder dissolved? Ask the students to find out what is done to make the consistency right.

Plenary

The students could write their own question loop, of five questions (or as many as in their table group). On the cards the students write the answer to a question and the next question, so that the first person to ask a question has to answer the last person's question. The loop can be given to another group to try. The questions should be on what they have learned in the last two enquiries about dissolving and saturation.

Questions could include the following. The answers given here are matched to the questions.

How do you make a solid dissolve faster?	Heat the water, or make the solid pieces smaller.
What happens when a solution is saturated?	No more solid will dissolve.
What does dissolve mean?	A solid disappears into a liquid.
If you heat the water does the solid dissolve faster or slower?	It dissolves faster.
How do you check results?	Repeat them and take an average.

Unit 4: More about dissolving – Mixing solids and liquids

The objectives for this lesson are that students should be able to:

- Find out if there is a limit to how much solid a liquid will dissolve

- Understand that a solution is saturated when no more solid will dissolve in the liquid

- Discover that some liquids form a suspension when mixed

- Present their results using ICT.

SB pp.52–53

Starter

- To show what saturation is, use a student volunteer to stand in front of the class. Ask them to hold out their hands. Start piling objects, preferably the same type, e.g. pens, into their hands. Tell the students not to move their hands. Eventually the student's hands will not be able to hold any more pens, but keep piling them on anyway. After several pens have fallen on the floor, stop. Ask the students what happened. Why couldn't any more pens be held? Relate to a liquid not being able to hold any more solid, so the solid starts to just drop to the bottom.

- Ask who has been caught in a rainstorm and got 'saturated'. What were your clothes like? How is being saturated with water like a saturated solution? (Neither will take any more!)

Explain

Can't take any more

When a solid dissolves in a liquid, it initially fills the spaces between the particles of the liquid. The level of the liquid does not rise. When all these spaces are filled, the solid no longer dissolves – and the liquid level begins to rise. (A curious anomaly is that, when a solid is first added to a liquid and dissolved, the level of the liquid may actually fall...)

Does particle size matter?

Some solids that dissolve have larger grains or crystals than others. The students could look at these through a hand lens or microscope and predict which material will dissolve most easily in water. This links with the activity in Things to do. Encourage students to explain their predictions and what they would observe if they carried out the experiment.

Things to do

That's the limit

This activity could be tailored to produce another full enquiry. It relies on the students planning their own investigation using their prior knowledge from the previous two enquiries. The type of substances that could be tested are baking powder, salt, sugar, bath salts, sherbet, etc. Try to use powders that produce transparent solutions, rather than materials like cornflower, which produce what is technically a suspension, rather than a solution.

Support

Some students will need help planning the investigation and making it fair. Encourage them to agree on a set volume of water to add the various substances to.

Extend

All students should observe that water can hold more of some solids before saturation than others.

Some students could investigate whether the change in volume of water produces the same pattern as the results from the dissolving sugar enquiry.

Record

If you chose to set this as an enquiry with the students working independently, then a full write-up could be produced.

If you plan the investigation with the students, then ask them to draw an annotated diagram of the set up, and a table and graph of results to show which solid dissolves most in water. This will be a clear record for the students when they revise.

Dig deeper

The Plimsoll line is a mark on the middle of the side of a ship that indicates how laden it is. As the density of water changes, depending on where you are in the world, the buoyancy of the ship also changes. This is related to the amount of salt in the water and the temperature of the water. So in warm waters, the ship will sit lower as the water is less buoyant. In more salty waters the ship will sit higher.

Did you know?

Some substances act like glue to make two immiscible liquids join together. This technically isn't a solution, but a suspension, as if it is left, the immiscible liquids will separate out again. Mix together oil and vinegar and show the students how they form two layers. Then add mustard powder and shake the mixture. This will form a suspension. Discuss with the students whether it is a solution or not (it isn't transparent).

Other ideas

Other solvents

The students could try using vinegar instead of water to observe whether the same substances that dissolve in water also dissolve in another liquid. If the students look at the contents list of some containers of liquid, they may have the word solvent on them. The students may also have heard of solvent abuse. This links to topics in Personal, Social and Health Education.

Presentation

The students could use a spreadsheet package to present graphs of their results from the activity.

The students could also perform a presentation to show what happens when you add a solid to a liquid, and that some solids are more soluble than others.

The students could role-play how a solution becomes saturated, in a similar way to the starting activities.

At home

Ask the students why they think that some food packets have instructions on to say how much solid to put in the water. Find out if it is better to add the water to the solid.

Plenary

Ask the students to produce a cartoon strip to show what happens when a solid dissolves and why some solids dissolve more than others in water.

Unit 4: More about dissolving – Unit 4: Review

The objectives for this lesson are that students should be able to:

- Check what they have learned on more about dissolving in this unit

- Find out how they are working towards, within and beyond the Grade 6 level.

Expectations

Students working towards Grade 6 will:

- recognize that a solid can be recovered from a solution by evaporation

- name some soluble and insoluble substances

- make predictions

- with help, investigate an aspect of dissolving and present results in a suitable table.

In addition, students working within Grade 6 will:

- recognize that solids remain in the solution when they dissolve and can be recovered by evaporation

- identify several factors that affect the rate at which a solid dissolves

- decide on an appropriate approach to testing their idea

- investigate an aspect of dissolving, presenting results obtained in a suitable graph and explaining what the results show

- measure volume and temperature accurately

- see if the evidence supports their prediction.

Further to this, students working beyond Grade 6 will also:

- present results in a line graph where appropriate

- use key vocabulary, e.g. solute and solvent when describing dissolving

- explain why it is important to repeat measurements and how to present repeated results when drawing a graph

- evaluate their repeated results.

Check-up

You could ask the students to try making coffee to see what the problems are with Hassan's coffee. He has used cold water and the coffee and sugar haven't dissolved, hence the sludge in the bottom of the cup. As he added the coffee after the water, he would also find that some of the coffee floated rather than mixed with the water. He may also have used coffee grounds rather than instant coffee.

Assessment

Use the Unit 4 assessment on WS 29 and WS 30 to check the students' understanding of the content of the unit. The answers are given opposite.

Name: _____ Date: _____

WS 29 Unit 4 assessment 1

1 Kavya and Javed are experimenting with solids and water. They put 2 teaspoons of each solid into a beaker and added 50 ml of water. They stirred each mixture and then left it for 2 minutes. These are the beakers afterwards.

a) What have Kavya and Javed done to make their experiment a fair test?
_____

b) What else should they have kept the same?
_____

c) Were all the solids they used the same? _____

d) How can you tell?
_____
_____

Answers

1

a They used the same amount of solids and water. They left the mixtures for the same amount of time.

b They should have kept the water temperature the same. They should have stirred each mixture the same number of times.

c Yes

d The solids all look the same

2

a Windowsill

b Salt/solute/sediment

c A saturated solution

d Sieving or filter

3 Filtering sieves out much smaller particles from water

Recall the introductory question.

The water should be boiling to help the sauce powder to dissolve and the noodles to soften. If the students want to eat the noodles quickly, they will need to allow them to cool. They could investigate the best ways to allow this to happen, e.g. a shallow dish, stirring, etc. They can also see what happens to the vegetables if they are left in the water. They soak up the water so they aren't hard and dry any more.

Set up a wall display of the classroom with labels showing: the best place to put a solution from which you want to recover the solid; where to put a solution from which you wanted to grow crystals.

Unit 5: Reversible and irreversible changes

The objectives for this Unit are that students should be able to:

- Understand that some materials are natural and some are made

- Learn how materials can be changed

- Understand and explain that these changes can be reversible or irreversible

- Collect evidence to test their prediction and explain their findings based on this evidence.

SB p.55 Science background

A familiar example of permanent or irreversible change is cooking. Even items that are mixed, such as cake ingredients, have been changed irreversibly. We can't get the eggs and flour back. Baking the cake results in a permanent chemical change. The creamed mixture bonds to become cake, quite different from the materials you started with.

Some changes are reversible. Some melting and solidifying activities can be reversed; others cannot. Candle wax can be melted and shaped, but not burned and reshaped because it changes chemically as it burns. The same is true of some food materials. While you can melt and reshape chocolate, melting butter loses its water content, and clarifies. This changes the butter; you can't get the yellow block back again.

Try, or think through, some everyday examples.

- *Make a cup of tea. Explain to yourself, in scientific terms, what you are doing as you make the tea. Which changes taking place are physical? Which are chemical? Which are permanent? Which are reversible?*

- *Open a bottle of pop. Is that a physical change? Or a chemical one? Is something new being produced or is this just a case of separation? Is there a gas being made or is it just coming out of the solution?*

- *Toast some bread. Is that a chemical change? Is it permanent? Can you reverse it? Burnt toast is carbon. That's a new material; so the change is a chemical one.*

- *Add a fizzy indigestion tablet to water. What happens? Is something new produced? Is that a chemical change? What gas is made?*

The difference between physical and chemical change is that physical change is only a change in form; the substance is still there. Sugar dissolving in tea is only a physical change; but baking a cake is a chemical change.

Language

Chemical reaction	Two or more materials together produce a new material.
Irreversible	Any change that is permanent. It's not possible to get back the materials as they were.
Reversible	It's possible to get back the materials you started with.

The Words to learn list on page 55 of the *Student Book* can be used to make a classroom display.

Resources

- *Material Changes* Reader

- Materials to mix, e.g. plaster of Paris and water, liver salts and water, bicarbonate of soda (or baking powder) and vinegar, washing soda and lemon juice, cement and water

- Water

- Measuring cylinders

- Burning candles, secured in safe trays of sand

- Tin trays or can lids held in pliers or tongs

- Glass jars of ice.

⚠️ Students MUST NOT touch soda crystals, cement powder or wet cement. Ensure they wash their hands after these activities. Students MUST NOT taste any of these materials or solutions.

Bright ideas

It is important not to equate reversible reactions to physical change, and irreversible reactions to chemical change. Some physical changes are irreversible – just try sawing your leg off and putting it back again! Some chemical changes are reversible – it's possible to heat blue copper sulphate crystals and watch them turn white as they lose water. Adding water brings the blue colour back and makes copper sulphate crystals again.

Skills check

Student need to:

- make careful observations and measurements

- collect evidence and see how good it is

- use their evidence to explain what they've found out

- use their evidence to predict something they don't yet know.

Some students will:

- suggest explanations for their observations from their scientific knowledge.

Knowledge check

- Students should recognize evaporation, condensation, melting, freezing and dissolving.

- They should also know that evaporation, condensation, melting, freezing and dissolving are all reversible.

- Finally, they should know what happens when materials evaporate, condense, melt, freeze and dissolve.

Links to other subjects

Literacy: Writing a non-chronological report, constructing effective arguments. Securing control of impersonal writing, e.g. by writing an evaluation of their enquiry.

Numeracy: Organizing and interpreting data: recognizing trends in data; presenting data in graphs and pie charts.

Let's find out...

The Unit opens with this question:

After the Diwali firework party, Hardip went round the garden. He collected all the fireworks he had watched the night before. 'I'm going to have another firework display tonight,' he told his mother. 'Not with those fireworks!' said his mother. 'Why not?' asked Hardip.

Link the question with any back garden display. Use it as an opportunity to emphasize the importance of firework safety. Hardip might just pick up a 'dead' firework that could harm him. But most will be empty tubes. Where has the firework powder gone?

Unit 5: Reversible and irreversible changes – Separation

The objectives for this lesson are that students should be able to:

- Learn how to get undissolved and dissolved solids back from water

- Make predictions about what they think will happen

- Explore what happens when different solids are added to water

- Display their results in a variety of ways.

SB pp.56–57

Starter

- Ask the students what they already know. Can you remember what happens when solids are added to water? What would you expect if you added sugar, coffee powder or marbles to water?

- Explain how to get an undissolved solid back from water. Remind them about filtering. Establish that they understand how a filter works.

- Explain how to get a dissolved solid back from water. Ensure that they are clear about evaporation and regaining dissolved solids.

- Ask them to explain what happens to some materials as they are heated and cooled. Begin to ask whether you can get the original materials back. Can you have the bonfire again?

- Remind them that burning materials can be dangerous.

Explain

Sand and salt

The separation of salt and sand is easy once you know how! There are two important steps which have to be considered in the correct order for success. This helps to review the students' understanding of the previous topic.

The first is to realize that sand and salt behave differently in water. Salt dissolves and sand doesn't. Adding the salt and sand mixture to water and dissolving the salt immediately separates them. But it doesn't get them back. For that, the students need to filter and evaporate, but in what order?

The second is to decide to filter first. They could evaporate the salt and sand together first, but they would end up with a mixture of the dry materials as before. Filtering removes the insoluble sand and then evaporating regains the soluble salt.

In practice, the sand is very salty – and the salt is quite sandy – but the principle is there.

Chocolates

Chocolate can be warmed and shaped and cooled. It is like a thermoplastic because it can be shaped when warm. In theory, chocolate is completely unchanged by heating. In practice, like butter, it is irreversibly changed. You will not get back the chocolate bar you melted but you can melt it – ideally in a bain marie to prevent burning – and shape it. Chocolate makers use moulds, and so can you. Or students can mix the melted chocolate with other materials – breakfast cereals or dried fruits – and make cakes and other treats. The chocolate will harden to hold its shape again.

> ⚠ Beware of dietary problems, diabetes and nut allergies. All work with food must be done in hygienic conditions.

Things to do

What happens with water?

Ask the students to add different solid materials to water and observe the outcomes. A fascinating change can be seen when water is added to cornflour, although not the other way round. Cornflour is a fine-grained flour used for thickening sauces and in custard powder and it can produce some very weird stuff indeed.

Let students spoon some cornflour into a cup. Add a little water and stir. Add a little more water and stir again. Stir slowly at first, then more quickly! You want to create a runny mixture. Now you will have a white putty which you can pick up and shape with your fingers. If you squeeze it, it changes to a liquid. You can make a ball from it and rest it on your hand. When is it a liquid? When is it a solid?

> ⚠ Plaster of Paris can get very hot when it is mixed with water, even without heating. Care is needed in handling this product. Try this yourself first. Use small quantities. Never put fingers into liquid plaster of Paris.

Record

Ask students to record in different ways. A Venn diagram could list the dissolvers and the non-dissolvers, with space in the overlap for the unexpected.

Support

Encourage students to predict before testing. How did their discovery match their prediction?

Extend

Discuss and explain the cornflour mixture. The tiny particles in solids are bonded together. The particles in liquids are free to move around. In this cornflour and water mixture, the particles are only loosely bonded. Squeeze or tap and they separate and the solid becomes a liquid. Cornflour and water is a thixotropic material.

Fire

Many students will have experienced fires and the fascinating remains – the ashes and twisted plastic, the metal fittings – that are left when furniture burns.

Burning is an irreversible chemical change that results in new products. Some of those products may be welcome but others will not be. Many products of burning are pollutants. Burning produces heat which changes other fireproof materials. Burning fuel around pottery items, for example, changes them irreversibly.

Rusting is a slow, long-term form of burning. Metal, in objects that rust, combines with the air to produce a new material. Iron becomes iron oxide. Water and oxygen are needed for this change, which is why metals rust in damp conditions.

Dig deeper

The fire triangle links three factors: fuel, oxygen and heat. If one of these three is missing, a fire will be extinguished.

Did you know?

Exploit any cookery activity to demonstrate irreversible change. The science involved is engaging. First, there are the ingredients – solids, liquids and in-betweens – that can be mixed, rubbed or creamed. Combining ingredients changes them; heating them makes irreversible changes and results in completely new products. Toast is different from bread; you can't get the bread back again. That's not true of adding materials to water. You can get the salt back again from brine, and taste the sugar in a fizzy drink.

> ⚠ Do not allow students to confuse science and cookery. It is good practice not to eat in science lessons. Do not allow students to eat uncooked materials, e.g. fondants made with raw egg white.

I wonder...

When candles burn, the wax – a solid fuel – melts to a liquid and this in turn evaporates or vaporizes into wax gas. Burning gas is what produces the light and heat from incandescent particles. But where does the candle material go? It is converted to water and carbon dioxide, and both are lost to the atmosphere.

Other ideas

Ask students to think about all the mixing and separating that might have been involved in preparing their dinner!

Presentation

Ask a group to pretend that they have just invented some new materials and want to sell them.

At home   WS 31

Ask student for ways of keeping cool on a hot day. How many involve evaporation?

Ask students to complete WS 31, consolidating understanding of changing materials.

Plenary

Separate salt, sand and water as a demonstration but do everything wrong! Ask the students to correct you.

Unit 5: Reversible and irreversible changes – Making new materials

The objectives for this lesson are that students should be able to:

- Explore what happens when different materials are mixed together

- Decide whether changes are reversible or not and explain how they know

- Take part in a scientific experiment to test their prediction

- Say if the evidence supports their prediction

- Explain what happened, using what they know about science.

SB pp.58–59

Starter

- Bring in a plaster model and some plaster of Paris powder. How has the model been made from the powder? Discuss the stages: making the liquid plaster, using the mould, waiting for the drying.

- Discuss mixing vinegar and baking powder. What is going to happen? Why will that take place? The mixing results in a model volcano! Try it:

  Add some red food colouring to some vinegar.

  Put a couple of teaspoons of bicarbonate of soda in a small plastic bottle.

  Pile sand around the bottle to make a volcano cone, leaving the top of the bottle uncovered. Now pour the red vinegar into the bottle and watch your volcano erupt!

The vinegar and bicarbonate of soda produce carbon dioxide gas. The reaction is irreversible.

The challenge

Sayyid has experienced an exothermic reaction – a reaction that produces heat, rather than needing heat to get it going.

What to do

Ask student to mix together some of these and describe what they discover:

- plaster of Paris and water: an exothermic reaction

- liver salts and water: the fizz is carbon dioxide; it neutralizes the acid of indigestion

- bicarbonate of soda (or baking powder) and vinegar: carbon dioxide

- washing soda and lemon juice: carbon dioxide

- cement and water: there is both a hardening and a chemical reaction.

> ⚠ Students must NOT touch soda crystals, cement powder or wet cement. They must not put their fingers in liquid plaster of Paris. Ensure they wash their hands after these activities. They must NOT taste any of these materials or solutions.

What you need

- materials to mix

- water

- measuring cylinders

What to check

Vinegar – a weak acid – reacts with the bicarbonate to produce carbon dioxide gas. This quickly fills the bottle, bubbling up and pushing the vinegar mixture out of the bottle top.

Demonstrate the production of this gas with another plastic bottle and a balloon. This time put the vinegar in the bottle and the bicarbonate of soda in the balloon. Stretch the balloon mouth over the bottle top. Then carefully lift the balloon so that the bicarbonate is tipped into the vinegar. The production of carbon dioxide will inflate the balloon with carbon dioxide gas. Use a thin vinyl glove in place of the balloon.

Support

Remind students to use small amounts of materials and to observe what they see and hear.

What did you find?

Record

Students should draw out a table for their results. They can compare their results and see what each has discovered.

Present

Ask students to show and explain their new materials to each other.

Can you do better?
WS 32

Show the students Sayyid's investigation results on WS 32. Ask them to complete the gaps in his table from their own knowledge and to draw conclusions.

Carbon dioxide is often a product of these reactions. It has a practical use in putting out fires.

Demonstrate a fire extinguisher. Float a nightlight candle in water in a jar. Light it with a long splint. Put several spoons of bicarbonate of soda or baking powder in the jar. Carefully, without dowsing the candle, add a little vinegar. The candle goes out because the mixture produces carbon dioxide. This gas is heavier than air, and pushes the air up and out. Without oxygen, the candle cannot burn.

Now predict

Both syrup and butter will melt. Melted butter is 'clarified' – it loses water and changes its consistency. Both changes are irreversible – although both melt and harden. So it isn't as clear cut as perhaps thought.

Other ideas

Introduce a novel new material: Borax (also known as sodium borate, sodium tetraborate or disodium tetraborate) is a mildly astringent disinfectant that you can buy from the chemist in crystal form. Add it to warm water, stirring until the water will take no more. Now it is 'saturated', add it, a little at a time, to PVA adhesive. Keep stirring as the glue absorbs the Borax. The PVA will become rubbery and can be shaped and modelled. The students can paint or varnish their models in two or three days.

Plastics are 'new materials'. Ask students to research the discovery and development of one plastic, e.g. bakelite, nylon or polythene.

At home
WS 33

Ask for a list of ten toys made from 'new materials', especially plastics.

Ask students to complete WS 33 on making new materials.

Plenary

Have a 'new materials' hunt round the school.

Unit 5: Reversible and irreversible changes – Irreversible change

The objectives for this lesson are that students should be able to:

- Find out and explain what happens when different materials are burned

- Understand that burning materials can be dangerous and that every possible precaution must be taken

- Discover what new materials are made

- Record and present their findings.

SB pp.60–61 Starter

- Show a photograph of a lighted candle (or the real thing) and ask what is going on. *Where is the fuel? Where is there a solid? Where is there a liquid? Where is there a gas? And where is there a burning gas?*

- Take in two candles, one new and one that has burned for some time. Compare the two. *Where have the waste products gone? Wouldn't you expect to see some ash?*

The challenge

The students have different ideas about what happens to the candle:

- Maybe things just burn away to nothing.

- When things burn, new things are made.

- Candles burn to give us a gas – or maybe some gases.

- If we can't see the gases, how can we tell they are there?

Ask the students what they will do. *Suppose one of the gases was water. How can you tell that there is water in the air?*

What to do

Clearly, the students must burn a candle! Firmly support the candle in a metal tray – foil cooking containers are cheap – with sand in it or use a stable 'tea light' candle. Ask the students to observe carefully. If they hold a tin tray or can lid or a piece of foil over the flame they will see soot collect; this is carbon, mostly wax that is incompletely burned.

A cold glass jar containing ice held over the flame will collect condensed water that has come from the burned wax. It is not easy to demonstrate the presence of carbon dioxide but if you invert a glass jar over a lit candle, the flame is extinguished not by a lack of oxygen but by a carbon dioxide 'blanket' that smothers the flame.

What you need

- burning candles, or tea lights, secured in safe trays of sand

- tin trays or can lids held in pliers or tongs

- glass jars of ice

What to check

Students may already know that carbon dioxide is a product of burning. You may find that if you put identical jars over two candles simultaneously, the taller candle will be extinguished first. This helps demonstrate that the carbon dioxide is what puts the flame out, though students may argue, reasonably, that the taller candle takes up more room and so that jar contains less air!

Carbon dioxide is odourless as well as invisible but other gases have a smell. Burn a perfumed candle. Although the perfume is invisible, it can be smelled throughout the room. Carbon dioxide can not be sensed in a similar way.

Support

Many students find it hard to grasp 'invisible products'. They are likely to conclude that the smoke from the candle is the carbon dioxide.

Extend

Challenge students to extinguish two candles simultaneously, using two different-sized jars.

They will have to think carefully about how fast the carbon dioxide can accumulate. Timing experiments with separate jars can produce accurate times for putting the jars over the candles.

Other candle-related challenges include:

- How are wick length and flame size related?

- How are candle size and burning time related?

- Can the dripping wax from burning candles be re-burned?

What did you find?

Discuss Farah's observations. Has she the evidence to justify her decisions?

Record

The students can write up their results as an annotated diagram of a burning candle. This should record the waste products of burning.

Present

The students could present their findings using ICT. Alternatively, ask students to imagine that they have invented a new candle product. They are to present this to the rest of the class who are the possible buyers. How will you sell your products? What are their advantages?

Can you do better?
WS 34   WS 35

Show the students Farah's report on WS 34. Ask them to explain the burning candle.

Use WS 35 to record their burning investigations. Food contains energy and oily foods like nuts burn fiercely. Rusting is a kind of 'slow burning' and a steel nail will rust in contact with air and water. Oiling or painting it will slow or stop rusting. Note that students may think that rust is bursting out of the nail.

Students could try burning postage stamp-sized pieces of other materials in the candle flame, using tongs, and observe what happens. Let them only use materials that you know are safe.

⚠ Some plastics and synthetic fabrics give off poisonous gases. Use tiny, harmless quantities. Avoid PVC – polyvinyl chloride. Follow the school guidelines on burning materials.

Now predict

Toasting is a process that converts the surface of bread to carbon. A small amount browns the toast, but a lot of carbon accumulates when the toast is burned! A checklist of things that happen when something is 'burnt' as opposed to heated could help explain – as suggested in the *Student Book*.

Other ideas

Ask students to research 'burning' words. For example, what do coke, coal, soot and ash mean?

At home
WS 36

Ask students to interview someone who uses an open fire. How is it made, lit and cleared?

Ask students to complete WS 36 which consolidates learning.

Plenary

Ask a group to pretend that they are cave people who have just discovered fire. They have to explain to the class why it is a great idea!

Unit 5: Reversible and irreversible changes – Unit 5: Review

The objectives for this lesson are that students should be able to:

- Check what they have learned about reversible and irreversible changes in this unit

- Find out how they are working towards, within and beyond the Grade 6 level.

SB p.62   **Expectations**

Students working towards Grade 6 will:

- use careful observation to describe a number of changes

- identify whether some changes are reversible or not

- plan to carry out a fair test.

In addition, students working within Grade 6 will:

- classify some changes, e.g. dissolving as reversible and others, e.g. burning as irreversible

- recognize that irreversible changes often make new and useful materials and recognize the hazards of burning materials

- make predictions and explain them, communicating these clearly

- choose their apparatus and decide how to use it

- identify the factors in an experiment

- collect their evidence and evaluate it. Does it support any prediction?

Further to this, students working beyond Grade 6 will also:

- explain that in some cases the new materials made are gases and identify some evidence, e.g. vigorous bubbling for the production of gases

- draw conclusions that are consistent with their evidence and explain these clearly.

Check-up

The barbecue gas will be used up, of course. Since its products are gases (water vapour and carbon dioxide) that are lost in the air, the cylinder will gradually become empty and weigh less. When it is empty, it will need refilling; most likely they will exchange it for a full cylinder.

Assessment   **WS 37**

Use the Unit 5 assessment on WS 37 to check the students' understanding of the content of the unit. The answers are given opposite.

Name: _____ Date: _____

WS 37   **Unit 5 assessment**

1 Look at these changes. Write 'R' next to Reversible changes, and 'I' next to Irreversible changes:

Evaporation   Melting   Solidifying

Condensation   Burning   Cooking

Freezing   Dissolving

2 Hassan is making a new pottery bowl. Write 'R' next to what he does that is Reversible, and 'I' next to changes that are Irreversible:

a) First he shapes the clay on the bowl.
b) Then he lets it dry.
c) He bakes the pot in the kiln.
d) He drops it as he gets it out.

3 Why are these good safety precautions when burning materials?

a) Fixing the candle upright in a metal tray of sand.

b) Doing up cuffs and tying back long hair.

c) Striking a match away from you.

d) Using very small amounts of test materials.

e) Holding test materials in tongs or pliers.

Unit 5: Reversible and irreversible changes   37

Answers

1

Evaporation	R	Freezing	R
Burning	I	Solidifying	R
Condensation	R	Melting	R
Dissolving	R	Cooking	I

2 a R **b** R **c** I **d** I

3 a Prevent it falling and starting a fire; metal does not burn; sand can be used to extinguish a flame.

  b Both could catch fire accidentally.

  c The burning match head could break off. This way it will not be shot towards your face.

  d Controls the size of the flame. Some materials might give off unpleasant or poisonous gases.

  e Stops fingers being burned.

The answer!

Refer back to the introductory question. The students will know that you can only burn fireworks once but they may not be so confident at giving you reasons. Look for an understanding that the firework chemicals have changed permanently and irreversibly. Much of the waste product must be gaseous, or you would need a steel helmet to watch a firework display!

And finally...

Produce a long, prepared candle with a wick at both ends, and a nail through the exact middle. Balance the candle by the nail between two drinking glasses. Put a saucer under each wick to catch the drips. Light both the wicks. Wax drops from one end, and the end rises. Now the other end drips, and that end rises. The candle rocks back and forth. The solid wax fuel becomes liquid and burns. Some fuel is lost as gas; both carbon dioxide and water gas, two products of burning wax.

Wax can exist as solid, liquid or gas. When wax burns, it produces carbon dioxide and water, and these are lost into the atmosphere. What about the liquid wax that runs down a burning candle? Ask students to explore – safely! – whether that still burns.

Unit 6: Forces in action

The objectives for this Unit are that students should be able to:

- Understand that forces act in pairs and can be measured in newtons (N)

- Find out that energy is needed to move something

- Describe the effects of friction and gravity on something they are trying to move

- Carry out scientific enquires and explain their results.

SB p.63 *Science background*

We don't usually think of forces in terms of doing nothing. Pushing a car down a road, pulling in a tug-of-war and twisting off a stiff lid are all examples of where the effort expended is obvious. We even talk about needing 'a lot of force' to move something. Forces in science are a little more subtle; they're at work even when we're not.

Students have already met the idea of a force being a push or a pull. Forces always exist in pairs. As one force acts on one thing then its equal but opposite partner force acts on the other. So your shoe pushes backwards on the ground as you walk and the ground pushes forwards on your shoe with an equal force. These forces are known as action and reaction. One cannot exist without the other.

Gravity is the invisible force that holds us on the Earth. Usually it is too weak to feel but it gets stronger the more stuff there is in something. The Earth is very, very big; it weighs six trillion trillion kilograms. Also, the Earth is very, very close to you because you are standing on it. The Earth's gravity is pulling down on you all the time. We call that pull your weight.

It was Isaac Newton who first proposed that everything that had mass also had gravity. Everything has a centre of this gravity, too. The Earth's centre of gravity is in its very middle, and so an apple will always fall towards the middle of the Earth. A tall object may have a high centre of gravity, and so it is easy to push over. Tall vehicles, such as double-decker buses, have all their heavy bits – the engine and axles – as low as possible, so that the centre of gravity is really low. A double-decker bus will lean a long way before it falls over!

Language

Action	The initial force.
Balanced	When two forces are equal and opposite so that there isn't any movement.
Forcemeter	A device for measuring forces in newtons (N). Also called a newtonmeter.
Gravity	The force of attraction between objects that pulls all objects towards each other. (Only usually noticeable when one of the objects has a huge mass, such as a planet.)
Kilogram	The unit of measurement for 'mass'. In everyday life it is used for weight: rather confusingly for students!
Matter	The 'stuff' that something contains.
Mass	The amount of matter that something contains. We measure mass in kilograms (kg).
Newton	The unit of measurement of forces (N).
Newtonmeter	The other name for a forcemeter as it measures in newtons.
Reaction	The partner force that works in the opposite direction from the action force. A 'reaction' is also when two materials/chemicals get hot, fizz, change, etc.
Unbalanced	When two forces are opposite, but aren't equal, so that there is movement in the direction of the force that is bigger.
Upthrust	The force pushing upwards on an object that is in a liquid (or a gas).
Weight	A measure in newtons of the force of gravity on an object.

The Words to learn list on page 63 of the *Student Book* can be used to make a classroom display.

Resources

- *Forces in Action* Reader
- A selection of forcemeters
- Digital balances
- Large containers for water, e.g. buckets, washing-up bowls or plastic aquaria
- A selection of elastic bands
- Hanging masses
- Stopwatches
- Tissue paper
- Thread
- Paper clips.

Bright ideas

Students often become confused between weight and mass. Remind students at every opportunity that weight is a measure of gravity measured in newtons and that mass is a measure of how much matter is in something and is measured in kilograms. Kilograms are used in everyday life to measure weight. One way to reinforce this is to discuss how your weight changes on the Moon. You feel lighter, but you haven't suddenly lost any part of yourself (such as a leg or arm!). Less gravity is attracting you to the Moon than on Earth, so less force is acting on you.

Skills check

Students need to:

- make careful observations
- make and repeat measurements
- collect evidence and decide how good it is
- notice patterns in results
- use their evidence to explain what they've found out
- use evidence to predict something they don't yet know.

Some students will:

- describe and explain the motion of some familiar objects in terms of several forces acting on them.

Knowledge check

Students should know that forces are pushes and pulls and that they act in particular directions. They know that we can't see forces but we can measure them and observe what they do.

Students know that friction is a force that slows things down and that friction between solid surfaces can be reduced with lubrication.

Students know that air resistance is a force that slows objects moving in air, and that water resistance is a force that slows objects moving in water.

Links to other subjects

Literacy: Reading and following instructions.

Numeracy: Measuring and comparing using standard units. Taking mean averages. Organizing and interpreting simple data in line graphs and tables. Using decimal numbers.

ICT: Using a multi-media package to combine text and graphics to make a presentation. Using spreadsheets to record and analyze data.

Design and technology: Evaluating produce effectiveness in terms of the elastic limits of various carrier bags.

PE: Looking at forces at work in sports.

Let's find out...

The Unit opens with this question:

Farida went to the market. She bought eggs, rice and fish and put them into a plastic carrier bag. As she lifted the bag the handles snapped and the groceries fell over the road. The fish and rice rolled down the hill and the eggs broke. Explain why that happened – as forces in action!

Discuss the problem with the students and encourage them to suggest solutions. Open up the discussion to include reasons why some things are heavy and others light. Does size matter or is it a question of mass? Can the students name any of the forces working in the shopping scene? Tell students they are going to find out about different forces acting on us.

Unit 6: Forces in action – Weight and gravity

The objectives for this lesson are that students should be able to:

- Understand and explain what gravitational attraction does to objects

- Find out how weight, mass and the force of gravity are related

- Measure force using a forcemeter and record their findings

- Explain the connection between mass and weight.

SB pp.64–65

Starter

- Deliberately drop a box of pens or bag of marbles. *Wouldn't it be better if things didn't fall to the ground? What would the world be like if things didn't drop?*

- Show the picture of Sir Isaac Newton on page 69 of the *Student Book. Do you know who this is? Can anyone remember why he's famous?*

- Explain that Newton was a scientist who wrote about forces around us. He was the first person to pull together all sorts of different scientific discoveries of how the universe worked. He through just a few simple laws governed the universe and he wrote them down to describe how objects move when they are acted on by force. Explain that this is what the students are going to learn about.

Explain

Gravity

Everything in the universe is made of matter. Newton believed that gravity was a force that attracted the matter in one object to the matter in another object. He wrote that the force of gravity that pulled objects to the ground on Earth was the same force that kept the planets in orbit around the Sun. Although it seems obvious to us today, this was groundbreaking science. Before Newton, some scientists believed that objects such as apples fell to the ground because they wanted to! Gravity acts over huge distances but is a comparatively weak force. The strongest forces are those acting over the shortest distance, for example, inside the nucleus of an atom.

How 'massive?'

Mass is the amount of matter or 'stuff' in something measured in grams and kilograms. The mass of an object is the same wherever you are, unless you change the amount of 'stuff' it is made of, e.g. chopping off a part of your body would change your mass!

Ask the students to think of two balls the same size, one made out of iron and one made out of wood. The iron ball has a greater mass than the wooden one, it's heavier and takes more effort to move. If you put the balls on a scale the iron might be several times the mass of the wood but wherever those balls were in the universe their mass, the amount of 'stuff' in them, would remain the same.

Weight

Weight differs from mass. Weight is what scientists call the force of gravity acting on an object and it's measured in newtons. When you buy a kilogram of apples, you are buying their mass, not the force of gravity acting on them.

Mass stays the same wherever you are but weight can change. The American astronaut Neil Armstrong couldn't bounce around on Earth the way he did on the Moon, so what had changed? His mass was the same, but the pull of gravity on him was less on the Moon than on Earth so he weighed less. The weight of something changes as you get further away from the Earth. This often confuses students so remember to flag up a scientific language alert!

Things to do   **WS 38** **WS 39**

Measure a force

Newtons (N) are named after Isaac Newton. A newton is a measure of the force of gravity acting on an object. 1N is the amount of force you'd need to pick up an average sized apple (about 100 g). This is seen as an easy-to-remember unit; Newton was inspired to recognize gravity as a universal force when an apple fell from a tree.

Encourage the students to examine their forcemeters and remind them of the mechanisms involved. The pull of gravity on an object suspended from the spring stretches the spring, moving the pointer. Students complete WS 38.

Record

The students can use WS 39 to record the weight and mass of a selection of objects. They can then make line graphs showing the relationship between mass and weight (they should get a straight line) and display them. Get them to use their graphs to predict the weight and masses at various points along the line.

Support

Students may need help choosing the right strength of forcemeter. Remind them that if they over-extend the springs in the forcemeters they could break the equipment. Let them practise predicting the weights of various objects and checking them on a digital balance until they get a feel for which meter to use. A mass of 1 kg on Earth has a weight of 9.8 N. Round this up to 10 N for less able students.

Extend

Students could investigate the weight of objects on other planets. Although we can't go there, we know that gravity is different on other planets and so we could work out the weight of objects mathematically (see ICT ideas).

Dig deeper

Let the students research why they wouldn't be able to stand up on Jupiter.

Did you know?

Our weight changes depending on the gravitational pull acting on us. Gravity keeps you on Earth. Ruggiero Boscovich, who lived in the eighteenth century, said 'Were it not for gravity one man might hurl another by a puff of breath into the depths of space, beyond recall for all eternity.'

I wonder...

On the top of a mountain you are further away from the centre of the Earth, so technically should experience less attractive force of gravity.

Therefore, you should weigh less. In practice this difference is very small.

Other ideas

Measuring mass

Ask the students to use secondary sources to investigate how people in the past measured mass and how these measurements have changed.

ICT ideas

Let the students use a spreadsheet to record the weight of objects in the classroom and then use the program to calculate their weight on the Moon or the planets. To find the weight on the Moon, enter a formula to divide the weight of the object on Earth by six.

Presentation

Ask the students to use secondary sources to find out about Newton's Laws of Motion. Encourage them to pretend to be his students and to make a PowerPoint presentation illustrating the laws, and set alongside experiments to demonstrate the principles involved.

At home

Ask the students to have a close look at a bathroom or kitchen scale that operates with a spring mechanism. Explain that these work in the same way as the forcemeters at school but this time by compressing rather than extending a spring. Ask the students to weigh themselves. What is your mass and what is your weight? What would your mass and your weight be on the Moon? Be diplomatic when asking for the students' weight! Don't force any replies!

Plenary

What is the magic number linking weight and mass? 10 (or if you're really brainy 9.81!) Play a quick number game to reinforce the link between mass and weight: 'My weight is 10 N so my mass is...?' etc.

Unit 6: Forces in action – Energy in movement

The objectives for this lesson are that students should be able to:

- Understand that a moving thing will carry on moving unless a force acts on it

- Find out what they need when they push, pull, throw or drop something

- Draw diagrams of their experiments, with forces represented as arrows

- Explore how forces can make things stop or change direction.

SB pp.66–67

Starter

- During a ball game in the yard, ask students if they can change the direction or speed of a ball they have kicked or thrown after it has left their foot or hand. They answer is simple. They cannot. They have transferred energy from their leg or hand to the ball and it will continue in the direction they kicked or threw until another force changes that.

- Stand a bicycle upright and push it towards a colleague who will catch it before it falls. Even without a rider on board, the bicycle should remain upright. You have transferred energy to the bicycle and with the help of free spinning wheels it will continue in the direction you choose until a mixture of friction and gravity slow it down.

Explain

The magic bicycle

Aleysha experiences the bicycle activity. Strictly, energy is transferred from her to the bicycle rather than being 'given'.

Adding energy

Taking the bicycle to the top of the hill gives it potential energy: that is, energy it possesses because of its state or position. The word 'potential' can be introduced once students are happy with the concept that you can transfer energy to the bike. Once the bicycle is rolling down the hill it has movement or kinetic energy. A compressed spring has potential energy; once it is released, it has kinetic or movement energy.

Energy chain

Energy can be neither created nor destroyed. So we can look back to the breakfast that Aleysha had that morning as the source of the energy that she transferred to the bicycle. That energy in turn came from the plants that made up her cereal; and these in turn harnessed the energy of the Sun to produce wheat.

Things to do

Forces in motion

A toy car at the top of a plank has potential energy. When it is let go, the force of gravity pulls to towards the centre of the Earth and so down the plank. The heavier the car, or the higher the plank, the greater the potential energy.

Record

These experiences can be recorded as pictures. Ask students to draw the forces involved as arrows. The head of the arrow should show the direction of the force. A push can be illustrated as an arrow 'pushing' the object, or as an arrow showing its direction.

Support

This is a difficult area, and understanding will come later. Abstract thought is needed to understand that a stationary object has forces acting on it. Absence of movement does not mean absence of forces. Ask students to think of examples of this; two Sumo wrestlers straining to push each other over, for example.

Extend

Some students will be challenged by the improbabilities of forces. They can explore more of these in books and on the Internet if they research Newton's Laws of Motion.

Dig deeper

Students can research more about forces and how they work.

Did you know?

A kicked football has two forces acting on it that slow it down and eventually bring it back to Earth. One is air friction and the other is the force of gravity. Even a football resting on the centre spot has two forces acting on it: the force of gravity pulling it down, and the force exerted by the ground pushing it back.

I wonder...

A bowling ball that is heavier has more energy transferred to it when it is first rolled. This means it will travel further and faster, hitting the pins harder and faster and so knocking more down.

Other ideas

More forces

Forces is a very difficult topic and the more experience students have of forces acting on them and on objects around them the easier they will find it to understand. However, it is also very exciting and challenging. They may find out from their own research that not only is the force of gravity pulling on them, but that they themselves are pulling on the Earth, albeit with a minute and almost insignificant force.

The Earth pushes back

It seems very unlikely that the Earth pushes back at a football resting on the ground. But you can demonstrate this using a ball and a metre rule. Use the metre rule to bridge the gap between the backs of two chairs. When you rest a ball on the ruler, you can see the ruler bend. This demonstrates the pushing force of the ruler. Bring the chairs closer together and shorten the ruler, and you can still see the ruler bend and imagine the force it is exerting. Bring the chairs very close together, and you can no longer see the bend but the ruler is continuing to exert a force.

Presentation

Ask students to use secondary sources to find out more about the extraordinary things that forces can do. They might explore the ideas of Galileo, for example.

At home

Ask the students to prepare some amazing facts to stun their families. Trying to explain what forces do and how they behave is a very good way of learning more about them.

Plenary

Finally, demonstrate with a spring and an elastic band that compressing and stretching some objects transfers potential energy to them which becomes kinetic energy when they are released.

Unit 6: Forces in action – Direction of forces

The objectives for this lesson are that students should be able to:

- Understand that several forces may be acting on an object at the same time

- Find out how to represent force size and direction to others

- Identify the forces that make different things work

- Explain how forces can be balanced.

SB pp.68–69

Starter

- Ask two students of about the same size to bring their roller blades, roller skates or skateboards to school. Wearing their roller blades or standing on their skateboards, set up a 'push-of-war' with the two students facing each other, palms together. What is happening here? Can we explain it in terms of forces?

> ⚠ Make sure you are in a safe environment with no obstacles and that the students are wearing protective safety helmets.

Explain

Pair up

Forces always act in pairs; exert a force and there will always be another pushing back. It's relatively easy to understand the influence of forces when we're talking about movement. A ball moves when you kick it; it moves in a particular direction and at a particular speed depending on how much force you use. Any object will stay still or keep moving in a straight line at a steady speed unless a force acts on it (a push or pull). We know that these forces can make something stop, move, or change direction, speed or shape. When we pull the chair from under the table we can see that the force of our muscles moving has caused the chair to move. So where is the partner force? Strange as it may seem, the chair pulls back with a force against us. The chair's force is weaker than our pull on it so it moves. If the force were equal to our pull, the chair would stay still. Remember that

forces have both strength and direction; forces can be balanced (in which case objects will stay still or move steadily) or unbalanced (in which case something will move or change).

Pulling on an elastic band is one way to demonstrate that forces act in pairs. When you pull on an elastic band you can feel it pulling back on your hand. Depending on how hard you pull you can exert a greater or lesser force on the elastic band or keep the forces between you and the band in balance.

The partner force will always be equal to the force at work but acting in the opposite direction. The initial force is called the action and the partner force is the reaction. If an object is pushed or pulled, it will push or pull equally but in the opposite direction. Balanced forces cancel out and so we often don't notice them. The book on your desk doesn't move so you're unlikely to think of the forces at work on it, but they are there. The downward pull of gravity on the book is balanced by an upward push on the book from the table.

You can demonstrate this with a blown-up balloon. If you push against the balloon you can feel the push of your hand. It you are holding it in both hands, your other hand has to push back to keep the balloon still. If you push the balloon against the table, you can feel the table pushing back to keep the balloon from moving. You can feel this even more if you place the balloon on the top of your head and push down. You can feel the push back through your head and neck.

Balancing act

Balanced forces also work in equal and opposite directions. When this happens we say that the forces are in equilibrium. You can see this easily in a tug of war. To begin with we have a state of balance where both teams take the strain and neither is exerting more or less force than the other, so nothing moves. Forces in balance on a moving object will keep the object moving at a steady speed and in the same direction. This is difficult to prove on Earth because we have the opposing forces of friction and resistance acting on our movement but in space you can see this in action. Once out of Earth's gravity and the atmosphere, rockets do not need to use fuel boosters as they will continue to move in the same direction unimpeded by air friction.

Things to do

Drawing forces

Two components make up a force: the first is its size, how strong a push or pull it is, and the second is its direction, which way it pushes or pulls. We draw forces as arrows. The length of the arrow shows how strong the force is and the way it points shows the direction of the force. Grade 6 students need to know how to represent forces as simple diagrams.

Record

Encourage students to draw examples of forces in action, moving and at rest. Ask them to add force arrows. Students should complete WS 40.

Support

Go through plenty of examples with the students, asking first where the movement is and in which direction something is travelling; and second, how strong the force is. Give simple examples to illustrate, e.g. pushing a wheelchair.

Extend

Once the students have identified the action force they should think about where the reaction force is and include this on their diagram.

Dig deeper

Students carry out research on Sir Isaac Newton and his laws.

Did you know?

These facts illustrate forces at work in natural and man-made contexts.

I wonder...

Forces can be combined together quite easily and drawn quite easily too. If one person tries to lift a heavy object then the force arrow will be a certain length and a particular direction. Add another person lifting at the same time and you keep the direction of force the same but double the strength (so double the length of the arrow).

Other ideas

Dance!

Encourage the students to make a sequence in dance or PE to show forces acting in pairs.

Air force

Balance a ping-pong ball in the stream of air from an upturned hairdryer. Can you describe the forces at work? What can you say about the forces when the ball remains still?

Gravitating toys

Take in a collection of toys and games that use gravity to work, e.g. slinky toys, yo-yos and Victorian flip ladder toys. Can you identify the forces that make these work?

ICT ideas

Let the students use a drawing program to add force arrows to pictures from clip-art. Use them as display materials.

Presentation

Encourage the students to devise a short play in which Isaac Newton explains and describes his discoveries.

At home

Refer students to WS 41. Ask the students to add the forces that are at work when we ride a bike.

Plenary

Display photographs of objects at rest and in motion on your interactive whiteboard or copied on to an OHP transparency. Challenge students to add force arrows to the pictures, explaining their choices as they draw.

Unit 6: Forces in action – Investigating upthrust

The objectives for this lesson are that students should be able to:

- Find out about the upward force water exerts on an object in water

- Understand that because of upthrust, objects in water weigh less

- Make careful measurements of force using a forcemeter

- Explain their results and any patterns they found scientifically.

SB pp.70–71

Starter

- Discuss the forces on a floating object. *What happens when we put things in water? Why do some things float and others sink? Let's try to find out and explain it in terms of forces.*

The challenge

Read the speech bubbles and What to do on page 70 in the *Student Book*. Has anyone done aqua aerobics? What about moving in water: is it easier to do some things in water than on land? The water lends some support to our bodies.

Objects float because they are less dense than water (or another liquid). If an object weighs less than its volume in water, it will float. If it weighs more than the equivalent volume of water, it will sink. Boats float because, containing air, their volume weighs less than the equivalent volume of water. The force of water surrounding a boat or any floating object, pressing to get that space back, is called upthrust.

What to do

Discuss how to tackle this investigation and what equipment might be needed. Make sure the students realize that the point of the investigation is to find the value of the upthrust of the water and not just the weight of the objects. Encourage the students to predict the weight of the objects they choose before they measure using a forcemeter.

What you need

- a section of waterproof objects that can be attached to a forcemeter (initially choose objects that you know will not float)

- forcemeters

- deep bowls of water (plastic fish tanks are ideal)

- lots of paper towels

What to check

Make sure the students are secure about what they are measuring and observing in the difference between the reading in air and water.

Support

Discuss how to take accurate readings using a forcemeter. The students may have to squat down so that their eye is level with the pointer on the forcemeter.

Extend

Students may enjoy the challenge of using a different liquid for comparison. They could try water saturated with salt and compare the results with pure water.

What did you find?

WS 42

Record

The students can use the table provided on WS 42 to record their results. Alternatively, they could use the idealized data given in the *Student Book*.

The students could convert their recorded data into a line graph. The data is continuous so a line graph is more appropriate than a bar chart. Less able students can present their results as a table.

Present

Encourage the students to look at their graph and 'tell its story'. Students should be able to work out a pattern in their results and to generalize a rule from the pattern.

By measuring the weight of an object in water then removing it and pushing upwards with their hand until the forcemeter reads the same in air as in water, the students will be able to feel the degree of support that the water gives.

Explain that the reading in air was measuring gravity or weight. It differed from the weight in water (remembering that the mass was constant) because of another force from the water. The force from the water acts in the opposite direction to gravity, i.e. it's pushing upwards. Students can feel this upthrust if they try to push a balloon or empty plastic bottle under the water. They should feel the water pushing these objects back at them.

Can you do better?

WS 43

Show the students Anya's investigation on WS 43. Ask them to complete the table – a single subtraction exercise – and then to answer the questions.

Until now the students have used objects that sink. What do they think the reading on a forcemeter would be if they used a floating object? Why?

The weight of a floating object measured in water is 0 N. This is because the force of upthrust exactly balances the force of gravity and the two forces cancel each other out. If the upthrust is less than the weight then the object sinks.

Now predict

Although the weight of objects might change in liquids because of the force of upthrust, their mass, the amount of 'stuff' in them, remains the same. So if your object has a mass of 200 g in air then it will still have a mass of 200 g underwater.

Gravity works the same anywhere on Earth, even through water. The difference in results was not due to gravity changing but the upward force of the water.

Encourage the students to explain their ideas through a demonstration and short presentation. You could organize this as a science fair for the whole school to come and see, or a school assembly. They could do this in groups.

Other ideas

Eureka!

Ask students to use secondary sources to find out about Archimedes, the Greek scientist who discovered the principle governing why objects float or sink.

Float a liquid

Liquids can float or sink in the same way as solid objects do. Pour equal amounts of golden syrup, cooking oil and coloured water into a jam jar and see what happens. The syrup sinks to the bottom of the jar, the oil floats on the top and sandwiched between the two is the water. This is because of the different densities of the liquids. Oil and vinegar are immiscible in the same way. Spilled oil floats on seawater. A liquid with a lower density weighs less than the same volume of one with a higher density, so a low density liquid such as oil will float on a higher density liquid such as water. Drop little bits of plasticine, plastic shapes, rubbers and coins into your liquid sandwich. If you're lucky you'll see that different objects float at different levels, e.g. a plastic brick might sink through the oil yet float on the water but a piece of plasticine will sink through the water but not the syrup.

Make a hydrometer

A hydrometer is used to measure the density of liquids. Make one from a lump of plasticine attached to the bottom of an empty ballpoint pen tube. You might have to fiddle with the ball of plasticine to get your tube to float upright but once it's stable it will float upright at a given height. Try your hydrometer in other liquids. The higher the hydrometer floats in the liquid the denser the liquid is. Demonstrate with water, white spirit and glycerine.

At home

Time to take a bath! Students can get very satisfactory results at home using ordinary kitchen scales to repeat Archimedes's experiments. Ask them to measure in grams rather than newtons, remembers that 100 g are roughly 1 N (200 g = 2 N etc.). Invite them to use various objects that float to displace water in a cup. What is the relationship between the upthrust felt by the object and the weight of the water it displaces?

Plenary

Is it easier to exercise in water? Explain that it should be because the upthrust of the water will support your body against the pull of gravity more than if you were on land.

Unit 6: Forces in action – Stretching springs

The objectives for this lesson are that students should be able to:

- Understand how adding masses to springs changes their length

- Find and explain the relationship between a spring stretching and the forces acting on it

- Make careful and accurate measurements of length

- Present their findings using ICT to explain the pattern.

SB pp.72–73

Starter

- Discuss bungee jumping. When you take a bungee jump, you trust that the owner of the equipment has calculated just how far a falling body – yours – will stretch the bungee until it reaches its elastic limit and stops you plummeting to the ground. The elastic limit of a material is the furthest it will stretch. It may stop stretching – or snap.

- Discuss stretching and squashing. Where else do we notice stretching and squashing? Standing on the bathroom scales, or weighing luggage with a spring balance, for example.

The challenge

Read the challenge on page 72 of the *Student Book* and discuss the ideas. *Do you agree with the students' ideas? Can more than one of them be correct? What do you think will happen?* Ask students to explore what happens to the length of a spring when weights are suspended from it. Suggest they make measurements so that they can look for a pattern in their data.

What to do

The students should decide on the measurement they are going to take and how they will record their results. They could compare springs of different lengths and thicknesses, or use similar springs.

If you don't have commercial or metal springs available you can make springs from paper and card. Cut a spiral out of the paper or card. You will need to test before the lesson, to see what the

maximum mass is that they can hold, as they will tear with heavy weights on them. This also allows you to have a wider range of variables in terms of thickness of paper or card, width of the band and length as well as number of spirals.

There are many springs in everyday life that can be used, from the springs inside pens and mechanical pencils to old bed springs!

What you need

- forcemeters

- retort stands and clamps, or secure hooks or poles to attach forcemeters to

- springs

- hanging masses; if you don't have these or enough to go round, use other non-standard masses such as marbles in a bag

- metre rules

What to check

Support

Some students may need help measuring and recording. It may be easier to mark the extension on a piece of card mounted behind the equipment and let the students measure from these marks. Help students to represent data collected as a line graph. Talk about the patterns in the graphs and ask students to make predictions from the graph, e.g. the length of the spring when another weight is added. Help students test their predictions, ensuring they do not over-stretch the spring.

Extend

Springs are often compressed as well as stretched. Try adding masses to a spring to 'squash' it, then how much it is compressed with each mass. Is the pattern the same as with stretching? Can the students predict the next step? You will need to have some quite large springs for this activity.

What did you find?

WS 44

The greater the force, the more an elastic material will stretch. An elastic material is one that can be stretched but will return to its original shaped provided the force applied is not too great (too much force and the elastic will deform or snap). As the elastic extends, more force is needed for the same amount of stretch. Eventually it will reach its elastic limit and no more extension is possible.

Record

Let the students use WS 44 to record their results and then transfer their data to a graphing program. Alternatively, they could use the idealized data given in the *Student Book*.

Present

The students could present their findings using ICT. Encourage them to look at their graph and 'tell its story'. Students should be able to work out a pattern in their results and to generalize a rule from this. Ask if gravity pulls more on a large mass than a small mass. Is there a relationship or connection between the weight and the stretch?

Can you do better?
WS 45

Ask students to review how good their evidence was. How would they tackle the investigation differently if they were starting again? Encourage them to use their graphs to predict the stretch of a spring at intermediate values they have not actually measured.

Can the students write a general rule to explain the outcomes of their investigations?

Look at the results on WS 45 and discuss them with the students. Ask them to complete the table.

Now predict

Before a bungee jump the participant needs to be weighed to find out their mass. The mass of the person has a direct effect on how much the elastic bungee rope will stretch. A heavier person will stretch a rope more than a lighter person using the same grade of rope. Heavier people may be given thicker ropes than lighter people.

By using a force arrow diagram you can see how well the students recognize the size and direction of the forces and it is a recognized scientific diagram!

Other ideas

Earthy pictures

Ask students to draw the Earth and the people living on it. Expect illustrations that do not represent the true picture; that the Earth's centre

of gravity is in its very middle, and that for people all over the Earth the centre is 'down'. Discuss this, using a globe. Establish that gravity is a force that pulls you towards the centre of the Earth.

ICT ideas

Ask students to compare the way that different objects, of the same size but different weights, fall. For example, compare film canisters with differing amounts of plasticine inside. They should find that – broadly – the weight makes no difference, and the objects – since they all have the same shape and so the same air resistance – hit the ground at the same moment. Use a light gate attached to a computer for accurate readings.

In a vacuum, or on the airless Moon, the canisters would fall at precisely the same rate. The classic demonstration of this, by astronaut Neil Armstrong dropping a feather and a hammer on the surface of the Moon, could be shown to them. Find it on the NASA website.

At home
WS 46

Ask the students to look in their cupboards for other items that might stretch and bring them into school to test them to their elastic limit.

Ask students to complete WS 46 which consolidates learning on investigations with springs.

Search around the home to find out where we use springs in everyday life. What types of objects do we find springs in? Ask the students to link the size of the spring with the job that it has to do, e.g. the spring in a pen will be small but the spring in a bed will be much larger – why?

Plenary

Put on some safety goggles. Blow up a balloon, and keep blowing it until it bursts! What's going on here in terms of forces? The more the elastic stretches, the more force you need to stretch it further; you have to blow harder and harder to get it to stretch just a bit more. Eventually it can't stretch anymore and bursts. If, however, you release the stretching force before it reaches its limit, what will happen? A balloon whizzing around a classroom is an example of Newton's Third Law of Motion, demonstrating action and reaction forces. Air jetting from the neck of the balloon drives the inflated balloon forwards.

Unit 6: Forces in action – Air resistance

The objectives for this lesson are that students should be able to:

- Understand and explain how air resistance and friction are related
- Find out that different objects areas are affected by air resistance
- Discover how friction can be overcome
- Take part in a scientific investigation and ensure that the test is fair.

SB pp.74–75   **Starter**

- Air resistance is a type of friction. Ask the students to run through the air holding pieces of card of different sizes in front of them. They might have done this before. If so, repeat the activity, this time asking them to predict what they think will happen and why they think that.

- Show some images of a range of cars and trucks. Discuss which will go fastest and why. Any that are streamlined will move through the air faster as they make a smaller 'hole' in the air. You could equate this to moving through water.

Explain   WS 47

Air friction

Friction is the force that slows down moving objects. All objects are subject to friction because, at a microscopic level, nothing is perfectly smooth even though it may appear to be. Friction can be reduced by lubricating surfaces with water, oil or grease.

When something moves through air, it has to push through the air particles. The air resists the movement and pushes back against it. As the object collides with the particles of the air it causes friction. The faster the object is moving the more collisions there are and the greater the friction. You can feel air resistance when you ride a bike and the wind pushes against you.

Leonardo's parachute

Leonardo da Vinci was famous for many scientific inventions and also artwork. He spent many years experimenting with flight and his best efforts involved not only parachutes but also attempting mechanical flight.

An open parachute has a very large surface. Demonstrate this by dropping a screwed up ball of paper and an open sheet at the same time and noticing how they fall at different speeds even though their mass is the same.

Parachutes are not only used for objects falling to Earth. They are used to slow down the speeds of drag racing cars and some landing aeroplanes.

Flat-fronted lorries have to push against a lot of air resistance as they move.

A sports car has a far more streamlined shape and will slice through the air with much more ease.

Falling fast

The speed at which an object travels is a measure of the distance it moves in a certain amount of time. So if you cycle at a constant speed of 20 km per hour, you will travel 10 km in 30 minutes. Scientists tend to talk about velocity rather than speed. Velocity is a measure of two things: how fast an object is travelling and the direction it is travelling in.

If a force continues to push or pull an object, its speed will steadily increase. This steady increase in speed is called acceleration. Acceleration measures how fast speed is gained, or in other words, how many more metres per second faster you go with every second that passes. A skydiver hurtling towards the ground accelerates as the force of gravity pulls him faster and faster towards the ground. The faster the speed increases, the greater is the acceleration.

Galileo couldn't prove his ideas described on page 74 on Earth because of the influence of air resistance, but on the Moon, where there is no atmosphere, astronauts were able to test his ideas by dropping a hammer and a feather together. Both hit the ground at the same time.

Things to do

Make a parachute

There are many possibilities for parachute investigations including variables to do with: the shape of the chute (circular, triangular, rectangular or even cone-shaped); the material it's made from, e.g. different grades of paper, plastics or fabrics; the surface area of the parachute; how long the strings are; the mass or position of the load and so on.

Find the fastest

As objects move through water they meet similar resistance to objects moving through air. An object collides with the particles of water as it pushes through them and this causes friction that we call water resistance. Because the particles in water are closer together than the particles in air, there are more to push out of the way. This is why it is harder to walk in water than in the air – you feel more 'friction' in water than in air. Streamlined objects with pointed, narrow shapes create less friction in water and move through it more easily; think about the shapes of fish or yachts.

Provide a range of substances in tall tubes and ask students which they think an object will fall fastest in. The substances could include water, air, wallpaper paste and vinegar. The thinner the liquid, the faster the object falls. This can then be linked to how 'thin' air appears to be compared to water. They can then experiment with how fast an object falls through thin wallpaper paste, based on its shape. Plasticine works well as you can shape it but keep the amount of plasticine the same. It's a good idea to tie a thread to the object so you can recover it. It is important here to link air as being another substance like water; that gases have particles that are very far apart and that's why we can move through them easily. The discussion about how the particles are closer together in water will help. If you have access to 'ball pools' then you could illustrate this with the students moving through varying numbers of balls.

Dig deeper

When an aircraft flies there are four main forces acting on it: the thrust of the engines which move the plane forwards; the frictional force of the air resistance opposing the thrust, which we call drag; gravity which pulls the aircraft towards the Earth; and lift. Lift is the upward force caused by the difference in airflow and pressure above and below the aircraft wings, which push the aircraft upwards. The pilot has to balance the forces of thrust, drag, weight and lift to keep the aircraft flying.

Did you know?

The faster an object travels through the air the more resistance there is and the more heat produced as a result of air particles colliding with the object. Meteors hitting the Earth's atmosphere become so hot that they break up. A space shuttle has a thermal protection system to enable it to withstand the high temperatures it encounters when it re-enters the atmosphere. However, the space shuttle *Columbia* was lost tragically in 2003 when this system broke down.

I wonder...

A free-swinging pendulum will not keep on moving and, in fact, the height of each swing will decrease with every movement until eventually the pendulum will stop. Gravity acts on the pendulum pulling it back to Earth at the height of each swing and this would in principle keep it swinging for ever. However, air resistance and resistance to bending in the string slows it down as it moves.

Other ideas

Make a kite

Students can have great fun with kites on a windy day. Use an old plastic carrier bag and tie a string to each handle. Leave the string about 10 m long and tie the other end to a metre ruler or a short pole. The students can then hold the ruler or the pole so they don't have the string sliding through their hands causing friction burns. Flying kits proves that wind and air has substance and force to move objects. You could also show video clips of hurricanes lifting objects that are normally considered too heavy for air to move.

ICT ideas

If you have one, use a pressure sensor or anemometer linked to an outside sensor and record wind force and wind speed in your area over a day. Help the students to put the results on a time chart.

At home

Ask students to draw something at home that is 'streamlined'. *Does it need to be this shape?* (e.g. even toasters can be streamlined!)

Plenary

Display a picture of a wind farm. Explain that these windmills are turned by the power of moving air. They pass on the energy from the wind to turbines, which make electricity for our homes. Air can provide a very powerful push that we sometimes underestimate.

Unit 6: Forces in action – Investigating aeroplanes

The objectives for this lesson are that students should be able to:

- Find out how air resistance acts in the opposite direction to the weight of a falling object

- Learn that streamlined shapes can reduce air and water resistance

- Calculate surface area accurately

- Record their data in a line graph and explain their findings.

SB pp.76–77 — Starter

- Come in with some homemade paper aeroplanes and throw them in the class. Ask the students to predict which they think will fly furthest.

- Share video clips of scientists flying paper aeroplanes.

- Share the fact that when scientists were making Concorde, they used paper models as prototypes to test their ideas – if scientists can make paper aeroplanes and throw them, so can we!

The challenge

Read the challenge on page 76 of the *Student Book* and discuss how the students could frame a question to investigate aeroplanes. There are many possible investigations and you could certainly try more than one. Do the students believe that the surface area of the aeroplane is the deciding factor relating to speed of descent? Do they have other ideas they could test?

What to do

Cut out a basic paper aeroplane and demonstrate how it works.

Brainstorm all the possible ways that the students could change the aeroplane. Write the ideas on the board; you may be surprised by just how many the students come up with. To reinforce the scientific method, it is a good idea for all to choose the same variable to change initially, e.g. the type of paper the aeroplane is made from. After that, each group or pair could test a different modification.

If you decide to investigate the surface area of the wings, you need to find a universal way of measuring this. Discuss what you mean by surface area. Should the wings by symmetrical or doesn't that matter? Could we increase the surface area by changing the wing shape? Do they have to be rectangular?

Making your aeroplanes from squared graph paper solves the measurement problem and make the task more accessible. Start with a super large aeroplane and reduce the surface area by chopping bits off, or else make several of different sizes. There are many, many possibilities and the discussion of the possible questions is as valid a use of time as doing the experiment itself.

What you need — WS 48

- paper aeroplanes

- scissors

- squared graph paper

- paper clips

- seconds timers

- measuring sticks or tapes

- a camera or video camera (optional)

Raising up the height of the students to release the aeroplanes will help with how far they travel. The higher they start from, the further the aeroplanes will travel.

What to check

Support

If all of your students are making modifications to the basic aeroplane design then all other variables must remain the same. The students need to be certain about just what they are testing. For example, if you change the length of the wings, should you do so by the same amount on both wings? There are endless possibilities here and most will give you interesting and valid results.

Extend

Extension work here lends itself to outcome rather than task. There are so many possibilities that more able students may be able to work through several.

What did you find?
WS 49

Record

The students could record their data onto WS 49. Alternatively, they could use the idealized data given in the *Student Book*. The students could create bar charts or line graphs from their information. These will differ according to the variables changed but the time in the air should always be recorded on the y-axis and the variable that is changed on the x-axis.

Present

Encourage the students to make a PowerPoint presentation to 'tell the story' of their graph. *Which was the most successful aeroplane? Which the least?* If students have used a camera or video to make a record of their investigation, they could import clips into their presentations.

Can you do better?
WS 50

Show the students the results on WS 50.

Ask students how good their evidence was. How could they tackle the investigation differently if they were starting again? Did their results in one experiment lead them to wonder about changing their method or their experimental variable? Are there other aeroplane investigations they'd like to try?

Some students might realize that in changing the surface area they are actually affecting other variables too but that these go hand in hand. You can't reduce the area without changing the shape and weight to some extent. How far do they think this affects the validity of their results?

Now predict

Look for an understanding that it is air friction that is affecting the flight of the aeroplane. Gravity is the force that is pulling the aeroplane to Earth and air resistance is the force that is slowing it down.

From their own results and those on the spreadsheet, students could make some estimations and sketch graphs to help explain their prediction.

Other ideas

There are other types of model aeroplanes on the market, e.g. those on which you wind up the propeller with an elastic band to see how the number of winds affects the distance flown.

ICT ideas

Students could record their results on a spreadsheet and use this to compile an average of several readings. Information from this activity could be entered into the graphing program and used to draw different types of charts. Remind students that all axes should have labels and that their graphs should all have titles.

At home

Ask student to find and collect examples of flying seeds.

Plenary

Find out about other objects that fly in nature, such as other seeds and animals.

Unit 6: Forces in action – Unit 6: Review

The objectives for this lesson are that students should be able to:

- Check what they have learned about forces in action in this unit

- Find out how they are working towards, within and beyond the Grade 6 level.

Students working towards Grade 6 will:

- identify weight as a force

- recognize that more than one force can act on an object

- measure forces using a forcemeter

- present measurements in tables and charts

- make predictions.

In addition, students working within Grade 6 will:

- identify that weight is a force and is measured in newtons

- describe some situations in which there is more than one force acting on an object

- draw diagrams to illustrate forces acting on an object

- use a forcemeter accurately to measure forces

- present measurements in simple line graphs and identify patterns in these and evaluate explanations

- decide whether to repeat their results.

Further to this, students working beyond Grade 6 will also:

- describe and explain the motion of some familiar objects in terms of several forces acting on them

- represent several forces on an object as part of communicating their understanding clearly

- explain why they repeated their results and evaluate these, identifying any results that don't fit the pattern.

Check-up

When something floats the forces acting on it (weight and upthrust) are balanced. The general rule is that if an object is lighter than the same volume of water then it will float. If it is heavier than the same volume of water then it will sink.

Although you may not be able to hollow out a brick you can make it float by attaching it to a larger surface area, e.g. polystyrene. This will make the brick lighter per unit area and keep it afloat!

Assessment   WS 51 WS 52

Use the Unit 6 assessment on WS 51 and WS 52 to check the students' understanding of the content of the unit. The answers are given opposite.

Name: _____ **Date:** _____

WS
52 **Unit 6 assessment 2**

6 A rubber duck is floating in water.
   a) What force is pulling the duck down? _____
   b) What force is pushing the duck up? _____

7 Anjali weighs a toy in air. It weighs 2 N. When she weighs it in water the reading is only 1.5 N. Explain why there is a difference in the two readings.
_____
_____

8 Rabab dropped a feather. It fell very slowly. What was the force that slowed the fall of the feather? _____

9 Look at these parachutes. Which parachute would fall slowest? Why?
_____
_____

A   B   C

10 Jamil was learning how to ski. His ski instructor told him that if he wanted to go faster he should crouch down low. Why did crouching make him go faster?
_____
_____

52   Heinemann Explore Science Grade 6

Answers

1 **a** All three arrows should point towards the centre of the Earth.

   b Gravity

2 **a** Force

   b Newtons (N)

3 25 N

4 It takes more force to move a greater weight.

5 The arrow representing the red team must be longer than the arrow for the green team.

6 **a** Gravity

   b Upthrust

7 The mass remains the same, but the weight of the toy is supported by the upthrust of the water.

8 Air resistance or air friction.

9 **c** The parachute with the largest canopy has the greatest surface area, and therefore the most air resistance.

10 It made him more streamlined by reducing his frontal size and his air resistance.

The answer!

Refer back to the introductory question. Farida had put a lot of heavy things in the bag which were all being pulled down by the force of gravity. The weight of the groceries pulling down was a greater force than the carrier bag could hold and so the handles snapped. The eggs broke because the force of them hitting the ground made them change shape (break). By now the students should be able to detail all the forces involved here, including the forces of equilibrium before the bag broke and forces of motion when the groceries rolled down the hill.

And finally...

Record a sporting event from the television. Back in school, encourage the students to do a commentary for an event about all of the forces in action! So, for instance, instead of David Beckham 'making a play for the goal but being brought down in the penalty box', you might have, 'Beckham, being beautifully supported in equilibrium with gravity, swings his left foot and, oh yes, overcomes the friction between his boots and the grass... here comes a pushing force in the shape of a defender, yes, he's going to act in the opposite direction. Which force will have the greatest strength? Over to you, Yasmin...'

Unit 7: Changing circuits

The objectives for this Unit are that students should be able to:

- Draw and explain a simple circuit, using the correct symbols

- Make a simple circuit and explain how it works

- Carry out scientific experiments on conductors and insulators

- Use their evidence to explain their findings and make predictions.

SB p.79   Science background

Students should already be familiar with constructing circuits and know that they need a complete circuit for electricity to flow. They should have made switches and know examples of electrical conductors and insulators.

It is far easier to show what electricity does than to explain what it is. Students will already be familiar with a range of circuits. We can build on this knowledge in Grade 6 and extend students' understanding of how a current is carried and what happens if the components in a circuit are not matched for voltage. Two major new concepts are introduced here: circuit diagrams and the symbols they are made up from, and resistance. Electrical resistance is a measure of the difficulty of the flow of electrical current through a material. It's what makes something a good or a bad electrical conductor. Altering the resistance in a circuit is the simplest way of varying the current in the circuit. You'll find this principle used in all sorts of domestic devices such as dimmer switches on lights and speed controls on toy electric vehicles.

Strictly, a single cylindrical battery should be called a 'cell'. Two or more cells form a 'battery'. But battery is in common use for a cell, and there is no need to be pedantic.

> ⚠ Bigger batteries are harmful of course and you can get a nasty jolt from a 12 V car battery. Even a small battery will tickle your tongue!

The battery pushes the electricity round the circuit. The circuit must be complete for the electricity to flow. All the components, linked in a complete circuit, are needed for a bulb in the circuit to light.

Look closely at a torch light bulb, when it is off! The wire filament inside is part of the circuit. (The glass bead in the centre of the bulb, holding the filament wires, is a different colour with each voltage.) The electricity flows through the bulb. Students are mainly asked to construct series circuits at this level and an understanding of parallel circuits is not a requirement. However, you may wish to extend your more able pupils in this direction.

Language	
Cell	A device that uses chemical energy to push an electric current.
Battery	Technically, the collective noun for more than one cell but commonly used to mean 'cell'.
Circuit	A closed path of conductors through which an electric current can flow.
Circuit diagram	A map of a circuit drawn using conventional electrical symbols.
Electrical conductor	A material that allows electricity to pass through it easily.
Electrical insulator	A material that does not allow electricity to pass through it easily.
Current	The flow rate of electrical charge. (The current is equal to the amount of charge passing a particular point per second. It is measured in amperes.)
Voltage	The push available to move charges from one point to another in a circuit; measured in volts.
Series circuit	An electrical circuit that provides only one path for the electric current to follow.
V	The symbol for volt.
Resistance	A measure of the difficulty of the flow of electrical current through a material.
Switch	A device that can be used to control or stop the flow of an electrical current.
Variable resistor	A component that alters the flow of electricity in a circuit, usually a resistance wire with a sliding contact so the length of wire can be changed.

The Words to learn list on page 79 of the *Student Book* can be used to make a classroom display.

Resources

- *Changing Circuits* Reader
- A selection of wires, crocodile clips, bulbs, bulb holders, wires (of varying thickness)
- A selection of batteries
- Nichrome or resistance wire
- Graphite or carbon rods. Leads from mechanical pencils are good.

Bright ideas

Inexpensive battery powered toys from discount stores and markets provide good sources of electrical circuits in action. Allow students to explore the circuits to find out how they are connected, and possibly to use the components in their own model making.

Knowledge check

- Students should understand that an electrical device will not work unless there is a complete circuit.
- Students should know that some materials conduct electricity and that others do not.
- Students should understand that different materials have different levels of resistance to electricity and that this can be altered.
- Switches can be used to break a circuit and stop the flow of an electrical current.
- Students should know that high voltage electricity can be extremely dangerous.
- Many students have difficulty with understanding that the current is the same at all points in a circuit. They think that the electricity will somehow have changed (usually become weaker) either side of a component.
- Students should know that electricians and scientists use symbols to represent components in a circuit.
- Students should recognize that circuits can be changed in a variety of ways.

Skills check

Students need to:

- recognize when to repeat measurements
- use their evidence to explain what they found out

- present results in table and in line graphs
- identify patterns in data
- use evidence to predict something they don't yet know
- recognize conventional symbols for some electrical components and construct some working circuits with specified components.

Some students will:

- interpret more complex circuit diagrams and describe the differences between wires usually used for circuits and fuse wires.

> ⚠ Warn students that they must never stick anything into a mains socket other than a plug and must never play around pylons or electricity substations.

Links to other subjects

Literacy: Reading and following instructions. Etymology and the origins of words.

Numeracy: Measuring and comparing using standard units. Organizing and interpreting simple data in line graphs and tables. Measuring and reading from scales.

ICT: Using a multi-media package to combine text and graphics to make a presentation. Using spreadsheets to record and analyze data. Using a light sensor.

Let's find out...

The Unit opens with this question.

Lightning is a type of electricity. Sometimes it hits, or strikes, your house. When it strikes it can make all the electricity in your house go off. Why does this happen?

Discuss the problem with the students and encourage them to suggest solutions. Note any misconceptions and probe to find the reasoning behind these.

Tell students they are going to find out about how we can alter circuits to make them work differently.

Unit 7: Changing circuits – Electrical circuits

The objectives for this lesson are that students should be able to:

- Find out how components are represented in a circuit and use these symbols accurately

- Draw their own circuit diagrams and explain how other circuit diagrams would work

- Understand how the performance of components in a circuit can be changed

- Explain how to design the most effective circuits for bulbs.

SB pp.80–81

Starter

- Display pictures of simple circuits.

- Challenge the students to draw these circuits on a piece of paper so that a partner can construct it from their instructions. Tell them they have three minutes!

- Keep counting down the time. Are they getting flustered? Not to worry, it was a trick. You knew they couldn't really do it. Can they think of an easier way?

- Explain that the students are going to learn how to draw circuits quickly and easily.

Explain
WS 53

Signs and symbols

We use signs and symbols everywhere in our daily lives to get messages across quickly and simply. Students may be able to identify many signs and symbols, e.g. road signs and markings, the school uniform, mathematical symbols, etc. Science has its own language of symbols too.

Circuit symbols

The students will have discovered from the Starter activity that drawing a realistic diagram of a circuit is time-consuming and difficult. Circuit diagrams simplify the circuits so that we can draw them more easily. Use WS 53 to teach the conventional symbols.

A circuit diagram shows the source of power, and the different components in a circuit and how they fit together. A circuit diagram uses a symbol for each component. Conventionally the power source is shown at the top.

Introduce the symbols for open and closed switches and encourage the students to predict what will happen in various circuits with switches open and closed.

All change

Students may already have a sound knowledge of symbols and circuits and how adding more batteries affects bulbs and their brightness. They may not have experimented with motors in a circuit. They should have made switches in previous years, recognizing that the electricity needs a complete circuit to flow round so that the components can work.

Things to do
WS 54

Draw a circuit

For this activity you should have plenty of equipment available and have already drawn out a selection of circuits with different components using WS 54. Remember the more components you use, the more wires you'll need to join them all together!

Support

Display a large poster-sized diagram showing circuit components and their equivalent symbols in a prominent place. Some students may need help with drawing straight lines or avoiding gaps in their circuits when joining two 'wires' on the page.

Extend

You might use this as an opportunity for more able students to try making parallel circuits. Very able students might be able to draw out a circuit diagram for traffic lights or doll's house lights.

Record

Display examples of real circuits alongside their diagrams.

How bright?

Use this as an activity to reinforce knowledge on changing the brightness of bulbs. Encourage students to draw a variety of circuits with bulbs and batteries altered. Students could predict the brightness of the bulbs, then make the circuit and test their predictions.

Support

Copy a rectangular circuit on a sheet of A3 paper and laminate. Leave gaps in your rectangle where components can be placed. Copy different component symbols on to paper, laminate and cut them out. Ask students to stick the symbols on the transparency, and so manipulate their circuits without the effort of drawing a new one each time. Don't forget to include some straight 'wire' symbols. This circuit could then be displayed in the classroom.

Extend

Students could write a set of rules for drawing circuits and display these in the classroom.

Changing components

This activity provides the students with an opportunity for 'free' experimentation with circuits. By the end of it, they should be considering how the number of components and batteries affect each other as a pattern, e.g. increasing the number of batteries will make a component work 'better' (bright/faster/louder). Increasing the number of components will reduce this.

Record

As a class, display a series of circuit diagrams on the wall showing different brightnesses of bulbs or other components and an explanation to go alongside each.

Dig deeper

Students should find out more about circuits and their construction.

Did you know?

Circuit symbols were invented for electricians, not for schools, and so the way we might draw them in school is slightly different from the way they are used in real life. Each symbol represents a component in the circuit. It is often frustrating for teachers to find that different books represent symbols in different ways. Older books may draw switches and bulbs differently. There are alternative ways of representing motors and buzzers too! The symbols given in the *Student Book* are the most common and up-to-date versions.

I wonder...

Current flowing through an object heats the object. The amount of current flowing through a wire in a circuit depends upon the amount of resistance it offers. If the resistance is very low, very high current can flow. A short circuit occurs when the large amount of current finds such a path of little or no resistance so as to produce a large amount of heat and cause a fire hazard.

Other ideas

ICT ideas

Use a drawing program to create a circuit drawing bank of symbols.

Presentation

Set up a complicated circuit on a board with switches and numerous bulbs that can be switched on and off in various orders. Write a series of challenge cards for the students to complete, e.g. can you switch on bulbs a and b without c being on?

At home

Ask the students to look at the lights in their homes. Are there any that can be switched on and off from different switches, up and down stairs perhaps? Can they imagine the circuit diagram for that particular piece of writing?

Plenary

Play one of the games above to reinforce students' knowledge of circuit symbols.

Unit 7: Changing circuits – Testing wires

The objectives for this lesson are that students should be able to:

- Find out how the length of wire in a circuit affects the brightness of the bulb

- Take part in a scientific investigation and ensure that the test is fair

- Make careful measurements and observations throughout their test

- Evaluate their findings and consider how to improve their investigation.

SB pp.82–83   Starter

- Display pictures of simple circuits with varying numbers of bulbs and batteries.

- Ask the students which bulbs will be brightest and why.

- We know that we can vary the brightness of bulbs in a circuit by adding or taking away batteries or by adding or taking away bulbs. Are there other ways of changing the brightness of a bulb?

The challenge

Read page 82 of the *Student Book* and discuss the students' ideas. Are there any that we can investigate? Can the students come up with any more variables to try?

Nichrome wire has high electrical resistance. It opposes or resists the flow of electrical current more than the copper wires we usually find in circuits. When an electric current flows through nichrome wire, heat is produced. You'll find the heating elements of kettles and electric fires have nichrome content. Warn students not to touch the wires when the circuit is on and for a time afterwards too, as they will be hot even if they don't look it.

> ⚠️ Do not touch the bare wire as it may be hot.

What to do

Have the equipment set up and give groups of students wires to test. Ask the students to predict what will happen to the brightness of the bulb as the length of nichrome wire in the circuit increases. Ask the students to try to explain their predictions before they begin. You should measure the brightness of a bulb in a nichrome-free circuit to give a baseline measurement for how bright the bulb is under normal conditions, for comparison.

What you need

- computer with light sensor attachment (optional)

- nichrome resistance wire

- metre rule

- batteries

- bulb

- connecting wire

What to check

If you have access to a light sensor then quantifiable readings can be taken straight from this. If you don't have access to this kind of equipment then you can still do the experiment but the results will be more subjective.

Support

Remind students that all conditions, apart from the length of wire, should be the same. Encourage accurate measuring and recording after each test. It may help if you draw the path the electricity is taking as some students may be confused by the 'excess' wire in the equipment. Explain that the current only flows through the wire in the circuit between the connecting crocodile clips and not along the whole length of wire.

Extend

Students should try testing another variable, such as thickness of wire.

What did you find?

Record

Students can draw out their own table to record results. If you have numerical data from a sensor you could transfer this into a line graph or scattergram.

Present

Let each group of students present their findings, perhaps using ICT.

Students should be encouraged to generalize from their results. They should find that the longer the nichrome wire in the circuit the dimmer the bulb glows. Nichrome wire has a much higher resistance to the current than copper so we can see differences more easily. The high resistance of nichrome wire means that it is more difficult for the current to move through it, and so only a small current flows through. The bulb will be less bright the more resistance there is in the circuit. The more nichrome wire there is in the circuit, the more resistance.

Can you do better?   WS 55

Use WS 55 to consolidate the relationship between the length of nichrome resistance wire and the brightness of a bulb.

To get a more accurate result you could measure the current in the circuit using a piece of equipment called an ammeter.

There are quite a few variables the students could test for, but in general the resistance of a wire depends upon the material it's made from, how long it is and how thick it is. For example, a short, thick copper or aluminium wire will have low resistance but a long, thin nichrome wire will have high resistance. You can explain it in terms of an assault course. It's easier for the electricity to move through a 'tunnel' that's short and thick than through a 'tunnel' or a wire that's long and thin.

Another visual image is to punch two holes in the bottom of a paper cup, one with a larger diameter than the other. If you pour water in the cup more will flow through the bigger hole (representing the thicker wire).

Now predict

The students will need to use at least two diagrams to illustrate what happens when you alter the length of wire in the circuit.

Other ideas

Hotting up

An electrical mains supply can force a large current through any wire. Wires such as nichrome or tungsten get hotter than lower resistance wires, such as copper, when large electrical currents flow through them. We can use this idea to our advantage in our homes. Nichrome wires in our toaster glow red hot so that we can toast bread; the glow from tungsten wires in light bulbs lets us see. How many more examples can you find? Ask students to make a display of appliances in the home where resistance is used.

ICT ideas

Challenge the students to use secondary sources and the Internet to research a biography of Georg Simon Ohm, the German scientist who first calculated resistance in wires.

At home   WS 56

Ask students to look at the cable connecting an electric cooker or a fridge to the socket on the wall. Compare it with the cable from a desk lamp. What differences do you notice? Can you think why one might be thicker than the other?

Ask students to complete WS 56.

Plenary

Display a series of circuit diagrams containing different lengths and thicknesses of wires. Challenge the students to predict which will have the brightest bulb in the circuit and explain why.

Unit 7: Changing circuits – Exploring conductivity

The objectives for this lesson are that students should be able to:

- Find out whether there are more conductors of electricity than insulators

- Understand that electricity can be dangerous and that every possible precaution must be taken

- Explain why metal is used for electric wires and why it is covered in plastic

- Learn how fuses work to protect them from electrical accidents.

SB pp.84–85   *Starter*

- Bring some electrical devices into the classroom, for example electric plugs and sockets. Explain that they are perfectly safe to handle because they're not connected up to the mains. Give a strong safety warning that once they are part of a mains circuit they can be dangerous, even lethal.

- Ask students why the devices are made of both plastic and metal. Can they imagine an electric plug made entirely of plastic with no metal parts? Why would it be no use? Can they imagine a wall socket made entirely of metal with no plastic cover or switch? Why would this be extremely dangerous?

Explain

Changing a plug

It is not appropriate to teach students how to change a plug, but you might explain in theory why the wires are different colours. Introduce the words conductor and insulator and talk about the functions of the metal and plastic parts of any plug.

Electricity flow

If the electricity current is strong enough, almost all materials will conduct it. But metals are good conductors, and that is why we use them in electrical circuits. Plastic is not a good conductor and so insulates us from the electricity.

You are a poor conductor

Emphasize the dangers of touching electrical devices with wet hands or when wet from the shower or swimming pool. While the dry body is a good insulator, wet skin can conduct electricity fairly easily and the results can be fatal.

Things to do

Conductors and insulators

Show students how to make an open circuit including a battery and bulb and three wires but incomplete, so that an object can be placed between the free ends. Ask them to explore a number of safe objects (not watches or electrical devices) to see which of them will conduct electricity and light the bulb. They should find that all metals are good conductors of electricity, and that imitations of metals – like some plastics – are not good conductors of electricity. There are exceptions to this, namely water and carbon (pencil lead). They have the ability to conduct easily, again because of their particle arrangements.

Protection

A fuse is a safety device that prevents a circuit from carrying too large a current. This way, it can prevent an electrical appliance from being damaged if there is a power surge and it also cuts down the risk of electrical fire. The working part of the fuse is the wire contained in the cartridge. It is made of metal with a low melting point. Different fuse wire carries different currents but if the current is too great for the fuse (and hence for the appliance), then the fuse wire will melt causing a break in the circuit, which stops the flow of electricity.

Circuit breakers have replaced fuses in many homes these days. There are switches that automatically break a circuit when too great a current is flowing.

Some devices are still fused, although these fuses are often in a bullet shaped container. If the fuse burns out or 'blows' then the wire has to be replaced, completing the circuit – very fiddly if it is dark and the lights are out!

Record

While students should not be changing plugs, they could record its wiring as a coloured picture, learning the colour code. Cards with the code are attached to new plugs. Most countries in the world use the European code (brown: live, blue: neutral, green/yellow: earth) but the USA uses a different code (black or red can be live, white: neutral, green or bare wire: earth).

Support

Little should be needed.

Extend

Students could prepare a safety poster for working with electricity.

Dig deeper

Students should find out more about the mains supply to their house and electricity generation.

Did you know?

There were no meters in the 1700s for measuring the strength of an electric charge. The charge was stored in a device called a Leyden jar, and if you touched it you might be knocked to the floor by the shock. But one early experiment measured how electricity flowed through the human body by getting a number of volunteers to hold hands and see how far through the chain the electricity could be felt.

I wonder...

Electricity will not flow through water, but adding salt to the water will make it into a weak conductor. Don't expect to light a bulb using brine, but you can make a circuit with salt dough 'wires'.

Other ideas

Conductors and insulators

Explore other materials that might be used as conductors and insulators. It could be possible to compare how well different materials conduct electricity.

Presentation

If the students' discoveries are displayed on the wall and a frame made from kitchen foil is placed around each one, it is possible to turn them into one big circuit and to light a bulb by pressing a switch.

At home

WS 57

Ask the students to look, without touching, at different places where they are protected by insulators from mains electricity. Ask them to find out why, in most cases, the light in the bathroom is operated by a cord.

Ask students to complete WS 57 as homework, revising electrical safety.

Plenary

Tell students that although air is a good insulator, electricity can jump gaps if it is sufficiently strong. Warn about the dangers of playing near electricity pylons and cables, or close to the wires of electric trains.

Unit 7: Changing circuits – Electrical resistance

The objectives for this lesson are that students should be able to:

- Understand and explain what resistance is

- Learn than different materials have different levels of resistance

- Find out how varying resistance in a circuit can change the performance of the components in it

- Make their own variable resistors and explain how they work.

SB pp.86–87 — Starter

- Display a picture of insulated copper wires.

- Ask the students why we cover copper wires in plastic.

- Students may respond that copper is an electrical conductor and plastic is an electrical insulator. *What do we mean why we say that? Let's investigate.*

Explain

Resistance

We know that electrical conductors are materials that allow electricity to pass through them easily and that insulators do not let electricity pass through them as easily. Given a high enough voltage many materials could behave as a conductor. In domestic situations we generally say that metals, with some exceptions like graphite and carbon, are good conductors while materials like glass, wood and plastic are good insulators.

Rubber, glass and wood have high resistance to electricity and copper, gold and aluminium have low resistance. Resistance is the ease with which electrons in the current pass through the material.

More means less

Electrical current is the flow of electrons through a conductor. In any circuit, the strength of the current depends upon the resistance of the components in it, e.g. the filament in a bulb or the wires in a buzzer.

Adding components in a series circuit (components connected in a straight line) will increase the resistance in the circuit; bulbs will become dimmer the more are added, motors will become slower, buzzers quieter. It's a bit like adding obstacles in a steeplechase. A runner who runs 100 m over flat ground will do a quicker more effective job than one who has to negotiate ditches and hurdles. So it is in a circuit. If all electricity has to do is flow through wires it will do so very effectively; if it encounters bulbs, motors or buzzers, then it will have a harder job. Surprisingly, motors may offers less resistance than light bulbs. So a motor may spin although a light bulb in series does not light up.

Which wire?

The metals with the least resistance to electricity are gold and silver but of course we don't use these in domestic wiring because they are too rare and expensive. Copper is plentiful, relatively cheap and has low electrical resistance so most household wiring is made of this metal.

Things to do

Varying the resistance

Although graphite does conduct electricity it has high resistance compared to copper wire. You can repeat the previous experiment using different lengths of graphite in place of nichrome wire to similar effect. Use lead from mechanical pencils.

Record

You could take a video recording of this experiment or digital photographs at the various stages.

Present

You could incorporate your photographs or video clips into a display showing how varying the resistance in a circuit can change the performance of the components in it.

Dig deeper

Superconductors are materials that offer virtually no resistance to the flow of current. As the temperature of metal decreases its resistance decreases also. When metals such as lead and tin are supercooled they become near perfect resistance-free conductors of electricity. They would be ideal for use in electricity supply cable, as the resulting cable would lose very little energy as the electricity was transported (about 3 per cent of energy is wasted this way). Superconductors would make your computer run faster, too, but they only work at really low temperatures (about $-270\,°C$) and as yet no one has made a superconductor that will work at room temperature.

The Baghdad batteries are quite amazing as no one realized what they did until about 80 years ago. The curator of the National Museum in Iraq where they were housed, examined them more closely and published his ideas in the 1940s. There is still some controversy about whether this interpretation is correct.

Did you know?

Hair-driers, toasters, light bulbs, electric fires and fan heaters, electric heating elements in kettles and on cookers are examples of using metals with high electrical resistance to change electrical energy into heat energy.

I wonder...

Students should be able to make the connection that materials which are good conductors will have a low resistance.

Other ideas

Ancient batteries

Research more about the original batteries and try to make one in the classroom. This could be by looking at the Baghdad batteries or looking at Voltaire's 'pile' which was a series of metal discs (you can use metal coins, alternating silver and bronze coloured ones) sandwiched with discs of fabric soaked in brine (you can use saturated salt solution). Touch crocodile clips to each end and

see if you can get a bulb to light up. If it doesn't, try making a taller pile -- it may be easier to lie this down in a row rather than build a tower as Volta did originally!

ICT ideas

Make a PowerPoint presentation with the class about electrical hazards in the home and how we can safeguard against them. You could include information about fuses and circuit breakers and the dangers of overloading sockets with too many appliances.

At home
WS 58

Electricity enters your home by a live wire and a neutral wire that are connected to a number of different circuits at the fuse box or trip switch. Most two-floor houses will have upstairs and downstairs lighting circuits, upstairs and downstairs power circuits (sockets), a circuit for a cooker and one for an immersion heater.

> ⚠ Students must NEVER touch the fuse box or trip switch, switched on or off.

Ask students to complete WS 58 revising their understanding of resistance.

Plenary

Ask the students if they know of anybody who has a radio that has a volume dial you have to turn. These have a sliding contact, which changes the length of a graphite track through which the current flows. (Graphite, you'll remember, is a conductor but one with quite high resistance.) In this way we can change the resistance gradually and reduce the volume. *If you have a radio like this at home, remember this the next time someone asks you to turn it down!*

Unit 7: Changing circuits – Unit 7: Review

The objectives for this lesson are that students should be able to:

- Check what they have learned about changing circuits in this unit

- Find out how they are working towards, within and beyond the Grade 6 level.

SB p.88 *Expectations*

Students working towards Grade 6 will:

- recognize conventional symbols for some electrical components

- construct some working circuits with specified components.

In addition, students working within Grade 6 will:

- suggest ways of changing the brightness of a bulb in a circuit

- draw circuit diagrams and construct circuits from diagrams using conventional symbols

- set up a circuit which can be used to investigate an idea

- use knowledge about electrical conductors and insulators to answer questions about circuits

- identify patterns in their results and explain these

- identify factors relevant to the investigation and use these to plan a fair test.

Further to this, students working beyond Grade 6 will also:

- interpret more complex circuit diagrams

- describe the differences between wires usually used for circuits and fuse wires

- use a model to explain clearly how electricity flows

- decide if the activity needs to have repeat results and evaluate these.

Check-up

The speed controller on Kemal's electric racing car set most probably works by using a variable resistor to alter the current in the circuit. When he squeezes the trigger in the handset a contact slides along the variable resistor, which will lower or raise the resistance in the circuit. Lowering the resistance will increase the current and make the car speed up; increasing the resistance will decrease the current and make the car slow down.

Assessment WS 59 WS 60

Use the Unit 7 assessment on WS 59 and WS 60 to check the students' understanding of the content of the unit. The answers are given opposite.

Name: _____ Date: _____

WS 59 Unit 7 assessment 1

1 Look carefully at this circuit.
Draw a circuit diagram for this circuit.

2 Look at these circuit diagrams.

A   B   C

a) Which circuit has the brightest bulb or bulbs? _____

b) Explain why this is. _____

3 Zinah connected a pencil lead between two crocodile clips. As she moved the crocodile clips to the ends of the lead the bulb grew dim. Explain why this happened. _____

4 What will happen to the brightness of the bulb in Zinah's circuit if she uses copper wires between crocodile clips? Tick the correct answer.
a) The bulb will be dimmer when there is a long copper wire.
b) The bulb will be brighter when there is a long copper wire.
c) The length of the copper wire makes no difference to bulb brightness.
d) There will be a short circuit and the bulb will go out.

Unit 7: Changing circuits   59

WS 60

Unit 7 assessment 2

5 Which of these are conductors and which are insulators?
Join them to the correct word with a line.

| metal screwdriver |
| plastic cup |
| knife blade |
| kitchen fork |
| rubber boot |

| conductor |
| insulator |

6 a) Why are the wires in your house covered in plastic?

_____
_____
_____

b) Why aren't the cables between pylons covered in plastic?

_____
_____
_____

60   Heinemann Explore Science Grade 6

4   **a**   The bulb will be dimmer when there is a long copper wire, but the effect will be slight.

5   Conductor: metal screwdriver
                        knife blade
                        kitchen fork

     insulator: plastic cup
                        rubber boot

6   **a**   To insulate them and prevent electric shock

     b   They are hanging in the air. Air is a good insulator, and the wires cannot be touched from the ground.

The answer!

Do you remember the question about the lightning? Trying to pass too much electrical current through wires or components that aren't matched to the power source will make the wires in them melt. Sometimes it isn't the house that has been struck by lightning, but the electrical substation instead. This will also have a series of much bigger fuses that electricians will need to reset. Warn students of the dangers of playing with mains electricity. Discuss why it is not a good idea to be out in a lightning and thunder storm where they might be struck, i.e. they may be killed as the amount of electricity passing through them would be very large.

And finally...

Electric racing cars are only one type of toy that uses varying resistance to work. Students may have other electrically powered toys that they could bring in to display. Talk about the role of electricity in each one. How does it change?

Answers

1   Accept any representation following conventional notation.

2   **a**   The middle circuit has the brightest bulb.

     b   This is because the two batteries combine their voltage to power just one bulb.

3   Accept answers that show an understanding that the pencil lead is made of graphite, which, although it does conduct electricity, is a poor conductor. The more graphite the electricity has to flow through, the more electrical resistance and so the dimmer the bulb.

Unit 8: Enquiry in context

The objectives for this Unit are that students should be able to:

- Plan and carry out scientific enquiries based on comprehensive evidence

- Explain how some famous scientists used enquiry skills

- Plan a burglar alarm and explain why it should work

- Collect evidence from enquiries and suggest ways of improving their work.

SB p.89   *Science background*

You are familiar with the business of scientific enquiry. You can quote the mantra, 'What am I going to change, what am I going to observe or measure, what am I going to keep the same?' You know all about fair testing, and how to control variables. Your school has adopted an investigational approach to science.

Investigation is not the only way to find an answer to a scientific question. In particular, it may not be the best way to answer an environmental or technological question. There have always been problems with planning investigations into plants and animals, and people. There are practical and moral limitations. You can answer some questions by observation alone.

Biological science demands different skills from the physical sciences. While physical scientists investigate by making changes, e.g., 'Let's mix this green stuff here with this foaming pink stuff here and see what happens', biological scientists are far more likely to observe – possibly over a long period – and draw conclusion from those observations.

Thus a biological scientist will explore pollution not by pouring a bucket of motor oil into a nearby stream and 'seeing what happens', but by comparing a polluted and a clean steam, or by observing the changes in a stream as it is polluted by circumstances. This approach involves asking questions, collecting and recording data, looking for patterns in it, and explaining their results, and the limitations of these results.

The enquiry into common cars offers an opportunity to practise this approach in a shorter time frame in order to maintain the students' engagement.

Technologists also work differently from scientists. While science is to do with finding out about the world that exists, technology is to do with creating something that doesn't. Since it's unlikely that your first crack at a new idea will be perfect, technology is also to do with adapting that idea in the light of evidence and experience to achieve a greater degree of success, and finally explaining that design in scientific terms and evaluating its effectiveness.

Language

Some general words are used with specific meanings in this unit.

Adaptation	In life sciences, to fit to your habitat.
Annotate	To label a picture or diagram.
Burglar alarm	A device to warn of, or prevent, theft.
Complete circuit	Electrical wires and components linked in a closed loop.
Conductor	Material that electricity can pass through easily.
Data	Information in number form.
Insulator	Material that electricity cannot pass through easily.
Sample	Part that shows what the whole is like.
Switch	Device to open and close electrical circuits.
Trend	General direction of pattern or graph.

Students should be able to plan an approach, to collect and record evidence, to use their knowledge to explain their results and to evaluate their evidence and say why it might be limited.

They should be able to describe a sequence of ideas; to link cause and effect (because, since); and to qualify their responses (it might, if we had). They should be able to use analogies to make something clear (a bit like this).

The Words to learn list on page 89 of the *Student Book* can be used to make a classroom display.

Resources

- *Obtaining and presenting evidence* Reader

- cooking foil

- thin squashy insulators
- several wires and crocodile clips
- bulbs in bulb-holders or a buzzer
- batteries.

Bright ideas

The Unit offers opportunities to use ICT to answer some of its questions, for example, a movement sensor or light gate might be the perfect switch to alert you of an attempted robbery.

Skills check

Students will need to:

- plan and carry out an investigation
- make careful observations and measurements
- collect evidence and see how good it is
- use evidence to explain what they've found out
- use evidence to predict something they don't yet know.

During this Unit they will practise:

- how to answer a scientific question
- deciding what evidence to collect
- handling data correctly
- explaining results from what they know of science
- deciding just how good their evidence is
- understanding the question they are answering
- making the right observations and measurements
- understanding the data they have collected
- using scientific words correctly
- having ideas of how to improve their work
- planning a burglar alarm using their knowledge of science
- testing their design
- improving their design so that it works better

- explaining how their design works
- evaluating their design, and other people's.

Knowledge check

- Enquiry is central to both the common car and the alarm activities. Information processing is also crucial to both activities. Not just the collection of information, but what you do with it, is critically important. How you choose which colour to count, and what you do to improve failing burglar alarms, are both areas for discussion.

- Arguing your case is one of the aspects of reasoning. While the suggested activities offer limited opportunities for innovation, it is possible that students could think creatively about the challenges; certainly they should evaluate their outcome.

Links to other subjects

Literacy: Writing a non-chronological report. Constructing effective arguments. Securing control of impersonal writing.

Numeracy: Organizing and interpreting data: recognizing trends in data; presenting data in graphs and pie charts.

Let's find out...

The Unit opens with this question:

'Look at all the caterpillars under these leaves,' said Aunt Layla to the children, 'They are all lined up – and all munching away. Why aren't there caterpillars on top of the leaves?' asked Aunt Layla.

'There are,' said Omar. 'But there aren't as many.' 'How do you know?' asked his sister. 'Because I've looked,' said Omar. 'Have you looked at all the leaves on the tree?' asked Aunt Layla. 'Of course not,' said Omar. 'Just how many leaves should we look at?'

The answer lies in sampling – testing a representative sample.

Unit 8: Enquiry in context – Common cars

The objectives for this lesson are that students should be able to:

- Find out how to answer a scientific question

- Decide what evidence to collect and carry out a scientific investigation to test their prediction

- Evaluate and explain their results from what they know about science

- Present their findings in graphs or charts, using ICT if appropriate.

SB pp.90–91

Starter

- Deciding on a sample size is a high level of thinking for most students. This can be illustrated with the cars activity. In reality it can be illustrated with many things.

- If you can see cars out of the classroom window, even just in the car park, you can make a sweeping statement about 'all cars are (whatever colour you can see)'. Ask the students if this is scientific and if it is correct.

- Have a bag of objects on the table. This could be full of socks, pencils, beads, coins, buttons or even pieces of coloured paper. Take out a single item, e.g. a piece of white paper. Say to the students that you think the bag is full of whatever you have pulled out, e.g. white paper. Ask them if they agree and why. Discuss what you have to do to prove whether you are right or not. Take out a second object, e.g. a piece of yellow paper. Now you could say that the bag is full of yellow and white paper or be even be more specific and say that there are equal numbers of yellow and white paper. Are you correct? Continue this until the students can relatively accurately describe what is in the bag. This shows the importance of either doing enough tests to get a reliable result, or having a big enough sample size to get a reliable result.

The challenge

Anya and Riya decide to count cars for five minutes.

What to do

There isn't a direct answer to this challenge, as it will be dependent on the local circumstances, but that's what makes it feel like a 'real' investigation. The answer is not yet known.

The students need to organize themselves so they can count the cars. It may be easier to assign a colour to each student in a group. These are probably best recorded as tallies in a table.

If you are unable to get out to carry out the survey, you could video a stretch of road at different times of the day. If you do this for two different stretches you have the added advantage of being able to compare the car colours, not only at different times of the day, but also in different locations.

What you need

- clocks or timers to time how long to count for

- clipboards to record the results

What to check

Carrying out surveys on traffic does mean leaving the safety of the classroom, but by running this activity at different times of the day, it is more manageable than choosing different locations at which to carry it out. You can't count every car, but the time needs to be set so that it is a large enough sample size.

Support

Some students may need help with organizing themselves and in creating a table.

Extend

Challenge more able students to produce charts and graphs of their data. They could also research the commonest car colour sold locally, asking all the students what colour cars their parents have. This could also be plotted on a local map, to see if there is any pattern of car colour and location.

A further survey could be to ask students what type/make of car they have in their family.

What did you find?

Record

Students can draw their own table similar to the one on page 91 of the *Student Book*. This could be used to produce a graph as well.

Combine the results of the groups' surveys into one table and make a class graph of the findings.

As a fallback, students could use the girls' data given in the *Student Book*. A bar chart can be produced of this data showing the number of car colours at each time of the day.

Present

There is a wide choice of presentations that the students could create, including illustrations, maps and newspaper articles.

Can you do better?

The girls only counted for 5 minutes. By counting for longer they may have got different results.

By looking at other colours of cars they may also have found a more common colour. They limited themselves so didn't look at all the evidence that was available. Sometimes this is useful in science, but only once you have already decided that there is reason not to include it. If the girls had carried out an initial counting exercise for a short time period of the total different colours of car, they could then have eliminated those that either didn't appear very often or at all, e.g. pink cars!

Predict

The obvious answer to this question is that there should be more people in the cars during the morning (going to work/school) and also at the end of the day.

Other ideas

How would we establish (for example) how much fruit or other food to buy or sell at a market stall? What factors do we take into account? How is the estimate made? Ask groups of students to observe a market stall – or fruit preferences – over playtimes. This is their 'sample'. What quantities of different products would they recommend stocking (remembering that fruit will not keep)?

Use a printed page for students to estimate how many letters 'e' or 'a' there are on the page. Why is it easier to count the letters 'z' and 'q'? If you use a computer-generated page you can automatically count a particular letter. For example, in Microsoft Word go to the Edit menu > replace, type in the letter then select 'replace all'. The program will tell you how many changes were made.

At home

Look around for examples of estimates: how much milk we are likely to need; how long the sugar will last; how many potatoes to peel; how many flowers on the curtains; etc. How will they tackle them?

Plenary

Discuss what other surveys could be carried out at home. Look for the commonest garden flower that grows in the shade.

Unit 8: Enquiry in context – Burglar alarms

The objectives for this lesson are that students should be able to:

- Plan a burglar alarm using their knowledge of science

- Evaluate other burglar alarms and consider how to improve them

- Test their design and explain how well it works

- Write a full evaluation of their enquiry and results.

SB pp.92–93   Starter

- When you press the button of a doorbell, you complete the circuit and the bell rings. Pressure switches are used in some kinds of burglar alarms. The pressure of the burglar's foot completes the circuit, and the alarm is set off. Discuss with students how this works; some may think that the push button is itself the bell or buzzer.

- Discuss the following circuit and follow the circuit through with the students: Electricity from a battery flows through a push switch when it is pressed or 'closed'. It reaches two coiled electromagnets, which are switched on and attract a hammer. The bell is struck.

- Demonstrate that this pulls the metal strip on the back of the hammer away from its contact on the right-hand side. This breaks the circuit and the hammer, which is on a springy piece of metal, snaps back to the right. This closes the circuit again – the electromagnets attract the hammer and the cycle is repeated.

- The switch opens and closes many times a second to produce the ringing of the bell.

The challenge

Pressure switches work when two conductive surfaces – in this case, two sheets of cooking foil – are brought together to complete a circuit. So that they shouldn't meet each other accidentally, but only when a burglar's feet rest on them, these two are separated by a squashable insulating material like sponge. Ah, you may say, but in that case, how can the conductors ever meet? The answer

lies in how you perforate the insulator. Holes in it should allow the two conductors to come into contact; but what pattern of holes, and where? That is the challenge.

What to do

Using chunks of plastic foam for insulators is not always very successful. Students seldom cut them thin enough. The best stuff to use is the grey foam sold in hobby shops as the underlay to model railway tracks. Sold in strips or rolls, it is very thin and may even be self-adhesive. It can be used to make a variety of patterns, so that it becomes possible to compare the effectiveness of alarms, not just to find that some work and some don't.

What you need

- cooking foil

- thin squashy insulators

- several wires – those with crocodile clips are best

- bulbs in bulb-holders or buzzers

- batteries

What to check   WS 61

Is the alarm visible? There should be no evidence of its presence.

Support

Students could use WS 61 to make an effective pressure switch.

Extend

Challenge the students to devise other unusual switches, e.g. a rain detector, a movement sensor, an earthquake detector!

What did you find?

Record

Students could record in the same way as Yasmin, writing a full evaluation with good and bad points and with plans for improvement.

Present

Let each group of students present their findings. Alternatively, invite the students to pretend to be sales reps selling burglar alarms that use a range of switches – 'Buy my alarm – it's reliable and sensitive – allow me to demonstrate!'

Can you do better?

WS
62

Use WS 62 to help students devise a burglar alarm for a lunch box. Using a simple see-saw like a ruler over a pencil is the trick. Taking the lunchbox makes the see-saw tilt and closes the switch.

Ask the students to review how good their evidence was. What could they do to improve their switch?

By creating an annotated drawing of their switch, the students might discover ways in which their switch could be improved.

Now predict

There are no opportunities for prediction in this Unit but there is a chance to evaluate, both their own ideas and other people's. Emphasize that the students must be sensitive to other people's feelings.

Other ideas

What other ways are there of recording and responding to a burglar's presence; door and window alarms, for example.

An object can be 'alarmed' so that lifting it opens – or closes – a circuit. Notice that some objects are heavy enough to keep a switch closed; that some are insulators and can hold open a spring-loaded switch. For example, wrap the jaws of a plastic or wooden clothes peg in tin foil, and connect a wire to each jaw with a drawing pin. As long as the jaws are held open, the circuit is broken by this spring-loaded switch. Any insulator can do that – the paper wrapping on a chocolate bar, for example. But 'steal' the chocolate and the jaws will come together, completing the circuit and setting off the alarm.

At home

Ask students to plan where they would put alarms, and what type of alarms they would like. It is not recommended that they discuss – publicly – their home security arrangements!

Plenary

The Red Hand team want advance warning of the approach of their rivals. How could this be arranged? Ask students to draw their own designs.

Unit 8: Enquiry in context – Thinking like a scientist

The objectives for this lesson are that students should be able to:

- Make the right observations and measurements

- Understand and explain the data they have collected

- Describe why repeating an enquiry gives more reliable results

- Come up with ideas on how to improve their work.

SB pp.94–95

Starter

- Show a picture of Einstein. Which of you will be the next Einstein?

Review the important science skills learned in this unit:

- understanding the question you are answering

- making the right observations and measurements

- understanding the data you have collected

- using scientific words correctly

- having ideas of how to improve your work.

Ask students where they used these skills.

Explain

Asking questions

Asking scientific questions can be hard. We ask questions all of the time, but developing these into a scientifically testable form requires practice, and a stimulus. No scientist asked a question without first 'playing' with whatever it was that interested them.

Provide students with a series of everyday objects that may also be thought-provoking such as stripy toothpaste, unusual bird feeders or objects from the kitchen they may not have encountered, such as melon ballers, or boiled egg slicers. There are many gadgets and toys like ratchet toy cars (ones you pull back and they move forwards on their own). Ask the students to come up with questions about them. It can be hard. Don't tell them what the objects are for – the imagination part is lost if you do!

Structure it a little further by asking them to come up with 3 types of question: a testable question

that they can find the answer to by testing out on the object; a question that they could find the answer to by researching the object and a question they think is very silly! Some students may need help with this so provide a range of question stems on the board, e.g. 'How does... '; 'What if... '; 'If I change... ', etc.

Often the silly question is a really good one to develop. A really good scientific question that is testable should identify the variables (this doesn't mean fair test) to be included, e.g. a student might ask 'How far will the ratchet car go?' They have identified what they are going to measure, i.e. how far the car will go, but not what they are going to measure. They could ask 'How far will the car go if I pull it back further?' This is a more scientific question.

The skills you use

Discuss the skills the students have been using. How have famous scientists used skills like these? Your television, your computer, your washing machine and maybe your cooker use electricity that comes to your house through cables. At the other end of those cables is a power station. The power station generates electricity for you to use. The power station uses the invention of Michael Faraday.

Before Faraday, people knew that bringing an electric wire close to a compass made the magnetic needle move. It was Faraday who first thought how this knowledge might help generate electricity, over 150 years ago. 'If electricity plus magnetism produced movement,' he thought, 'perhaps movement plus magnetism will produce electricity.' He tried moving a magnet near a wire. Sure enough, it generated a current. As long as you can make the magnets move – using a steam turbine, moving water or the power of the wind – you can generate electricity.

So, Faraday combined thought (prediction) with action (moving magnet near a wire) to make a discovery that changed all our lives.

Do the students have any science stories like this that they could tell the class?

Things to do

WS 63

Observation

Help students to develop their observational skills of plants in other ways. Some examples follow.

Play an exploration game (rainbow chips) to help them appreciate the wealth of colour in the environment. Ask them to collect tiny samples of colour – leaves, petals, twigs, small pebbles – to make a 'rainbow'. Alternatively, they could collect all the shades of one natural colour.

To learn more about the unique features of plants, they could play 'What am I? In turn, they write a plant name on a card, turn it over and ask their friends to identify it from a maximum of 20 yes/no questions.

To help them experience the uniqueness of natural objects, create (out of the students' sight) an indoor nature trail. Tie a string between two chair backs; tie natural objects to it by short strings, like a washing line. Blindfold a student and ask him or her to walk along the string and identify the objects by touch.

Record

Students could write about science in general terms – a day in the life of a scientist, what scientists really do – challenging the crackpot Professor image! Use WS 63 to make notes on some scientists.

Support

Encourage students to look closely, using aids like hand lenses as appropriate. Microscopes magnify but huge magnification is not the ideal. Magnification must be appropriate to the object you are looking at and what you want to see. Even low magnifications can make a huge difference and show you what you want to see. You may want to see a spider's leg but not every hair on it!

A magnifying glass will usually enlarge things two to three times. A simple microscope will enlarge 20 times. This is enough for most purposes.

Hold a magnifying glass close to your eye. Move the objects towards your eye until it is in focus. Combine maximum light with maximum clarity!

Extend

Encourage students to use microscopes. Most microscopes reverse the image and your movements. Choose a microscope that keeps the image the right way up, and that moves the image in the same direction as the object.

Science

Why study science? Students should be beginning to understand that science is a way of developing:

- scientific knowledge
- problem-solving skills
- attitudes
- practical skills.

What they learn should have:

- scientific importance
- human importance
- social and economic importance
- personal importance.

They should be developing as independent learners.

They should recognize the importance of practical work.

They should understand the unique contribution of science to their education.

They should be aware of the importance of ICT in their education.

Did you know

Scientists need many skills including those of careful observation and measurement. They need to be able to communicate and present what they have noticed, so that others will believe what they say they have found out. Some questions, such as the one about common cars, can be answered only by a survey, but others such as which is the best paper aeroplane, can be both researched and experimented on. Often how a question is asked defines how it is to be answered. Sometimes even the silliest sounding questions are the most useful ones to investigate.

Plenary

Plan, together with your associated secondary school, an activity that the students can start in primary schools and complete in their new school.

Unit 8: Enquiry in context – Unit 8: Review

The objectives for this lesson are that students should be able to:

- Check what they have learned about enquiry in context in this Unit

- Find out how they are working towards, within and beyond the Grade 6 level.

Expectations

Students working towards Grade 6 will:

- put forward ideas about what needs to be done to answer a question

- with help, plan what to do

- make relevant observations and measurements and record these appropriately

- suggest explanations for their observations and communicate these using scientific language.

In addition, students working within Grade 6 will:

- make a suggestion of how to investigate a question and plan what to do

- decide what evidence to collect and whether to repeat the measurements

- make a series of observations or measurements appropriate to the task and record these appropriately

- identify patterns in results and any results that don't fit the pattern

- explain these results clearly using scientific knowledge and understanding, and scientific language

- evaluate the method used and suggest improvements

- predict, and see if the evidence supports their predictions.

Further to this, students working beyond Grade 6 will also:

- plan what to do and how to use available resources effectively

- suggest limitations of the data collected or the product made and how these could be reduced.

Check-up

Ask the students to discuss the following statements in small groups and share their answers with the rest of the class:

'It looks as if every apple tree in the orchard has bugs,' said the farmer.

'I have to cut both wires from the pressure pad,' thought the burglar.

'I believe that the whole country is behind me,' said the president.

'I expect the battery is flat, so the alarm didn't work,' said the policeman.

'I've spoken to five people and they are all against the new road,' said the protester. 'Popular opinion is on my side!'

How can these statements be justified? What evidence might confirm or change these statements? What tests or sampling might provide evidence?

Assessment   WS 64   WS 65

Use the Unit 8 assessment on WS 64 and WS 65 to check the students' understanding of the nature of being scientific. The answers are given opposite.

Name: _____   Date: _____

WS 64   Unit 8 assessment 1

When you do an experiment you have to tell others your results. You need to explain them. But which is the best way?

1 Rani asked her class what their favourite colour was. She wanted to share this with her friends. She had these choices:

a) Tally chart	b) Table	c) Block graph
Object / Count / IIII IIII II	What I Change / What I measure	
d) Line graph	e) Venn diagram	f) Written report
	A B	

Which should she use for favourite colours? Why is this way best?

_____
_____
_____

Name: _____ Date: _____

WS 65 Unit 8 assessment 2

Scientists often repeat their investigations. They may take several measurements of the same thing.

Hammad was flicking a paper ball across the table. He thought that he could flick a smaller ball further. He made different sized balls and flicked them across the table. He flicked each ball 3 times. These are his results:

Ball diameter (cm)	First flick (cm)	Second flick (cm)	Third flick (cm)	Average (cm)
1	13	15	17	
2	25	18	26	
3	28	35	37	

2 a) Complete his table of results. Add the results together. Divide by 3.

b) What is the pattern in his results?

_____

c) Which two flicks did not fit the pattern?

_____

d) Why should he do these flicks again?

_____

e) Why is it better that he repeated his flicking and took an average?

_____

Unit 8: Enquiry in context — 65

Answers

1 The tally is a natural way to collect survey information, as the question choices are already set, and it is only the responses being counted.

The table bar chart could be used to present the tally.

The line graph is not appropriate as the data is not continuous – one colour does not lead into the next, and the Venn diagram is for grouping and sorting, so again not appropriate.

Award 1 mark for explanation of which to use.

2 a Table completed should have: 15; 23; 33

b Award 1 mark for noticing that the biggest ball went the furthest.
Award 2 marks for the comparative pattern along the lines of, the bigger the ball the further it travelled.

c 18, 27

d Accept answers based on the recognition of the odd-looking results from each set should be repeated again (1 mark).
Accept explanations based on the results being very different from the others so not being 'trusted' or reliable (1 mark).

e Accept answers based on the average helping to get rid of the odd results that have already been noticed. This makes the results more reliable as the more times you do it, the more likely you are to get consistent results.

The answer!

Refer back to the introductory question. Well, how many leaves should they look at? Perhaps it's more important that they take their sample from different places – the top and bottom of the tree, the side branches and close to the trunk. That way their sample may be more representative.

And finally...

Encourage the students to make a display of their discoveries – and their inventions – for parents' evening. They could challenge parents to enter the 'alarmed' classroom, or to estimate the number of 'e's on a page of the newspaper!